P.M. WHEELWRIGHT   ASSOCIATES
125 CEDAR STREET,   N.Y.,N.Y. 10006

UNIVERSAL GRID

STRUCTURE

Z - MARK ENTRY - SCALE OF BODY

MARK EXIT

EXTENSION OF INSIDE/OUTSIDE

PRODUCTION OF ZONE (PROGRAM)

LOCAL SPATIAL MANIPULATOR
(STAIR)

SPACE DEFINER (DINING)

OBJECT DEFINER (ONYX)

TEXTURE

FLARED TOP & BOTTOM

MIES VAN DER ROHE

David Spaeth

Preface by Kenneth Frampton

RIZZOLI
NEW YORK

For Anthony and Sloan

First published in the United States of America in 1985 by
RIZZOLI INTERNATIONAL PUBLICATIONS, INC.
712 Fifth Avenue, New York, NY 10019

Designed by John Bradford
Set in Bodoni Book by Roberts/Churcher

Library of Congress Cataloging in Publication Data

Spaeth, David A.
   Mies van der Rohe.

   Bibliography: p.
   Includes index.
   1. Mies van der Rohe, Ludwig, 1886–1969.   2. Archi-
tecture, Modern—20th century—Germany.   3. Architecture,
Modern—20th century—United States.   I. Title.
NA1088.M65S54   1985   720'.92'4   84-42768
ISBN 0-8478-0563-8 (pbk.)

Printed and bound in the U.S.A.

CONTENTS

PREFACE: The Unknown Mies van der Rohe

"Advancing technology provided the builder with new materials and more efficient methods which were often in glaring contrast to our traditional conception of architecture. I believed, nevertheless, that it would be possible to evolve an architecture with these means. I felt that it must be possible to harmonize the old and the new in our civilization. Each of my buildings was a statement of this idea and a further step in my search for clarity."
—Ludwig Mies van der Rohe
A personal statement, 1964[1]

Ludwig Mies van der Rohe has long been recognized as one of the four founding masters of twentieth-century architecture and, like the other pioneers of the Modern Movement, his work divides into two distinct periods. The most fertile part of his career was to extend from the mid-twenties to the mid-thirties, when economic depression, political reaction, and the crises culminating in the Second World War finally eclipsed the material and spiritual bases of an exceptionally creative epoch.

The postwar period, which for Mies began in Chicago in the early forties, brought with it a new sobriety; that is to say, a general feeling on the part of the pioneers that the determination of the constructional procedure should now play a more expressive role in the determination of modern form, irrespective of whether this was to manifest itself in *beton brut*, as in the case of Le Corbusier, or in exposed timber cladding, as in the American work of Gropius and Marcel Breuer. Mies, for his part, opted for the exposed steel frame and for the architectonic potential of the rolled steel section, which had long been an indispensable element in modern American building. It is significant, however, that Mies derived his particular use of the trabeated frame from the German industrial building tradition—from the countless steel and brick infill factories which populate the Ruhr and from the refinement which this idiom underwent at the hands of such architects as Fritz Schupp. This mode of construction ought more properly to be considered as building, that is, as *Bauen*, rather than as architecture, and as Spaeth suggests in his discussion of Mies's I.I.T. campus, Mies was all too aware that different building tasks (or that is to say, different institutions) required different levels of elaboration and enrichment. In this connection he stated, "Every building has its position in a stratum—every building is not a cathedral,"[2] and elsewhere, "There are good roses, but all plants cannot be roses; there are also good vegetables."[3]

Mies's relevance today lies in the emphasis he placed upon structure and the importance he attached to the act of building as a poetic gesture. His famous aphorism that God is in the details is only part of the story, since the sublime for Mies resided in the quality of the material itself and in the revelation of its essence through construction. His memory of the circumstances under which he selected the onyx for the interior walls of the Barcelona Pavilion reveals better than any other anecdotal passage the respect he felt for all material and for the way in which this factor alone has influence over the final result:

". . . since you cannot move marble in from the quarry in winter because it is still wet inside and would easily freeze and break into pieces, we had to find dry material. Eventually I found an onyx block of a certain size and since I only

had the possibility of this block, I made the pavilion twice that height and then we developed the plan."[4]

Mies's sensitivity in this regard was not reserved just for luxurious materials but applied to quite ordinary, everday building products, to brick, for example, of which he said: "Architecture begins when two bricks are put carefully together. Architecture is a language having the discipline of a grammar. Language can be used for normal day-to-day purposes as prose. And if you are very good you can be a poet."[5]

Mies never demonstrated this last assertion better than in the brick houses he built in the twenties and early thirties: in the Wolf house built at Guben in 1926, in the Hermann Lange and Esters houses which were both realized near Krefeld between 1927 and 1930, and finally in the Lemcke courtyard house realized in Berlin in 1932. In all these instances the position assumed by Mies is less avant-gardist than that manifested in his famous Brick Country House project of 1923, where the spatial expression and formal composition owe much to the Neoplastic architecture of the Dutch de Stijl movement.

This difference is perhaps all the more striking because, as Werner Blaser was to demonstrate later in his painstaking reconstruction of the bonding logic of the Brick Country House, the tectonic means adopted in each case was basically the same, that is to say, bonded solid-wall brick construction with all the dimensions and proportions worked out in accordance with the basic brick module. As Johnson was to remark of this period: ". . . he calculated all dimensions in brick lengths and occasionally went so far as to separate the under-fired long bricks from the over-fired short ones, using the long in one direction and the short in the other."[6]

It is interesting to note the subtle variations that occur in the tectonic of these houses—the fact, say, that the Wolf house, which is the most spatial of the three, employs the Flemish as opposed to the English bond which is used in the other two houses, or the fact that a double soldier course plus a header coping course is used throughout on the upstand walls of the Wolf house whereas the upstand in the Hermann Lange and Esters houses is simply finished with a thin metal coping. At the same time a certain lapsus occurs in the principles of structural rationalism in all three houses, since the steel lintels spanning the horizontal openings in the brick walls are totally concealed behind brick stretcher courses.

These three works, together with the second Ulrich Lange and Hubbe houses projected in the thirties, are particularly relevant to our understanding of Mies today, since they display his early work in a curiously ambiguous light, one which is as much touched by traditional expression as it is influenced by the avant-garde. This is borne out not only by Mies's curious remark that he would have liked to use much more glass in these houses but also by the spatial planning of the houses.

What is perhaps the greatest surprise in the Wolf, Hermann Lange, and Esters houses is the total absence of the free plan, which is soon to appear as a completely developed form in the Barcelona Pavilion and Tugendhat house. The only hint of a free plan in the earlier houses is a form of *en suite* planning, so that while every room is in principle a self-contained volume, the main living spaces are united with each other by a series of double doors. In the Wolf and Esters houses in particular this axial connection staggers across the orthogonal plan to impose a diagonal spatial movement throughout the total living area.

This contradiction between closed volume and a more dynamic form of spatial unity is even more evident in the second Ulrich Lange and Hubbe house projects, with Mies gradually shifting the emphasis back toward the free plan. Yet even in the Hubbe house, which is in many respects the most fluidly planned work of Mies's brick house period, the overall spatial dynamic is contained by the bounding courtyard walls, which serve to stabilize the composition and give it a feeling of Olympian calm.

This evident opposition between traditional and avant-gardist spatial concepts finds its most articulate expression in the Tugendhat house, where the main living volume is a fully glazed, freely planned spatial continuum and the bedrooms are closed, traditional volumes illuminated by pierced windows. The capacity of the retractable plate-glass wall to transform the Tugendhat living room into an open-air belvedere only serves to heighten this contrast.

I have singled out Mies's brick houses not only because they remain the least known and least publicized aspect of his career (despite Wolf Tegethoff's exhaustive study[7]), but also because they afford a revealing standpoint from which to reassess the total achievement of his life. It is interesting to note in passing that it is exactly these brick houses which are usually glossed over in all the standard monographs on Mies, although Philip Johnson's famous study is a singular exception in this regard.

The brick houses are important because they show Mies, under the influence of the *Neues Bauen* movement, projecting works which are altogether closer to Hannes Meyer's Trades Union School in Bernau of 1930 than one would have otherwise thought possible. The use of standard steel sash windows in these houses is symptomatic. It is a mode of expression and a form which one does not usually associate with Mies, and it is this same standardizing impulse which determines the continuous gridded glazing applied to the non-public floors of Mies's Reichsbank competition design of 1933.

Contrary to the vulgar view of Mies as the cold aesthetician of corporate architecture, these brick houses of the late twenties and early thirties continue to assert themselves as models for achieving a normative urban fabric, as valid today as when they were built or projected over half a century ago. The same can be said for his Afrikanische-strasse workers' housing in Berlin, a work which, while pleasantly mellowed by time, still seems as human a solution to the problem of mass housing as when it was first completed in 1925.

These undervalued Miesian residential models seem rele-vant today for at least two reasons. In the first place they return us to the possibility of producing a well-built, stable, and yet rather anonymous inner-urban fabric, a mode of domestic building which is both durable and unobtrusive, a kind of "almost nothing" which we do not commonly associate with Mies. This sublime "suburban" architecture seems to fuse with nature without disappearing. In this regard Mies's largely unrealized courtyard house projects of the thirties offer a self-effacing, well-serviced environ-ment which even today would still be capable of meeting the needs of modern life. In the second place they demon-strate the intrinsic quality of craftwork, as in the prototypi-cal "classical" furniture pieces that Mies was to build in the Berliner Metallgewerbe during this same period. These exquisite pieces posit a beauty which is dialectical rather than conventionally rhetorical; that is to say, they deliber-ately juxtapose gleaming machine-tooled, chromium-plated surfaces with delicately worked, traditional glove-leather upholstery, this last material replete with all of its burgher associations.

One further unacknowledged aspect of Mies's career seems worth remarking on before bringing this brief introduction to a close. This concerns the closeness of his early work to the "ineffable" sensibility of Russian Supermatism. De-spite Mies's denial that the Russian avant-garde had any impact on his work ("I was very strongly opposed even to Malevich," he was to tell Peter Blake in 1962),[8] there remains an uncanny affinity between his work and the visionary projects of the Neo-Suprematist architect Ivan Leonidov. Aside from the play of tinted, opaque, and oblique glass in the Barcelona Pavilion and the Russian color scheme adopted in the 1927 Exposition de la Môde, designed with Lilly Reich, a number of other exhibitions staged by Mies in the late twenties point in this same direction, above all the glass industry suite designed by Mies for the Stuttgart Werkbund exhibition of 1927. We need only to read Johnson's account of the materials em-ployed in this exhibition to sense that this work came close to Kasimir Malevich's famous *White Square on White* painting of 1918. This is clear from the list of finishes employed: ". . . chairs, white chamois and black cow hide; table, rosewood; floor, black and white linoleum; walls in etched clear and grey opaque glass."[9]

Two projects for unbuilt "great rooms" from Mies's late career testify to the persistence of this sensibility. Both of these employ a mixed technique of collage and photomontage which resembles the representational means employed by Leonidov. I have in mind the interior perspectives for an auditorium and a convention hall of 1942 and 1953 respectively. Where the former consists of a collage of wood veneer and metallic papers laid over a photograph of one of Albert Kahn's aircraft factories, the latter uses marbled paper to represent the stone-veneer screen walls bounding the enormous column-free hall. This marbled perimeter, interrupted by latticed cross-bracing in steel, seems to be of the same order as the photomontaged convention crowd occupying the floor beneath the vast space-frame roof.

A similar spirit is detectable in the canonical types of Mies's late career, that is, in the high-rise tower and the long-span exhibition hall, the first exemplified by 860 Lake Shore Drive, Chicago (1951), and the Seagram Building, New York (1958); the latter finally realized in the New National Gallery, Berlin (1968). A Suprematist aura lingers about these works even today, above all perhaps in the towers—in the Seagram Building, in the fusion of the bronzed mullions with the brown tinted glass, as though they were both transmutations of the same basic material; at 860 Lake Shore Drive, in the "condensation" and "expansion" of the projecting mullions of the Chicago curtain wall as one moves around the pinwheeling twin slabs. Set in discretely tended grounds against the infinite expanse of Lake Michigan, these closely mullioned slabs, together with the steel-frame terrace houses which Mies realized in Lafayette Park, Detroit, in 1963, serve to recall the floating, silent, curtain-walled prisms of Leonidov's Magnitogorsk proposal of 1930.

All of this has a long history in Mies's work, so much so that Mies's minimalist standard of "almost nothing"—*beinahe nichts*—seems to be a fusion of two equally romantic visions: the ineffable, misty light of Caspar David Friedrich's landscapes and the ethereal silence of Malevich's Non-Objective world. The way in which this synthetic vision was to qualify Mies's lifelong reinterpretation of the *Schinkelschüler* tradition is perhaps most unequivocally evident in the chromium-plated columns which he employed in the Barcelona Pavilion and the Tugendhat House. A more condensed compound metaphor in the history of modern architecture would be hard to find, since these columns so evidently combine in a single tectonic element a plethora of complementary yet contradictory references. These references are at one and the same time traditional and avant-gardist; while, on the one hand, the highlights of the cruciform chromium column clearly evoke the fluting of the typical classical order, on the other, they also serve to dematerialize the form, to bring it to the point of being "almost nothing." This preoccupation with dematerialization runs as a *leitmotiv* through Mies's career, as though the modern machine-tool mirage was the last refuge of the sublime. The regional origin of this sensibility was perhaps never more touchingly revealed by Mies than when he remarked toward the end of his life: "I remember the first time I ever went to Italy. The sun and blue skies were so bright. I thought I'd go crazy! I couldn't wait to go back to the north, where everything was gray and subtle."[10]

The New National Gallery in Berlin, the last realized building of his life, was a homecoming for Mies in more ways than one, since in this structure he was to reconcile at last the conflicting poles about which his work had always been divided: on the one hand, an impulse toward the infinite spatial continuum of the avant-garde, and on the other, a profound respect for the tectonic tradition of architecture. These opposed values were never more at variance with each other than in the main volume of Crown Hall at I.I.T., where the continuity of an uninterrupted ceiling plane totally repudiates the tectonic articulation of the perimeter structure. Despite their evident abutment on the plated steel cornice which caps the roof line, the perimeter structural mullions lack all grounding on the interior since in perceptual terms they appear to extend infinitely beyond the plane of the suspended ceiling.

This dilemma, which occurs in various forms throughout Mies's American career, first approaches resolution in the concrete space-frame of the Bacardi Building, which Mies projected for Santiago, Cuba, in 1957. Now, for the first time, the ceiling plane assumes the form of an egg-crate supported on eight columns set in from the corners of a square plan. This paradigm, translated into steel for the unrealized Georg Schäfer Museum (1968), finally becomes the *parti* for the pavilion of the New National Gallery in Berlin. This reconciliation or "homecoming" depends upon the dual nature of the Berlin space frame, for while it asserts its status as an infinite plane in space, it also establishes its intrinsic tectonic order through the intersecting lower flanges of the rolled steel sections of which it is composed. This egg-crate grid, divided into sixteen square modules in both directions, receives columnar support four modules in from its extremities on all four sides, four chords of the space-frame coinciding exactly with the column heads.

Here, one might say, the infinite space field of Suprematism finds itself sustained by the precepts of the classical, that is to say, by the cruciform columns which carry the egg-crate roof. With these supports the wheel comes full circle and Mies returns to his Neoclassical reinterpretations of the late twenties—to the cruciforms which supported the infinite planar ceilings of the Barcelona Pavilion and the Tugendhat house. The differences, however, are as significant as the similarities, for while these columns, like their predecessors, are patently metaphors for the "lost" columns of the antique world, they are, at the same time, tectonically removed both from actual classical precedent and from the dematerialized supports of Mies's earlier period. For now the columns are all too material, and the chromium-plate illusion of fluting has been replaced by the real modeling of what are, effectively, four T-sections in steel welded into a cruciform figure along a single vertical seam. The column in Berlin can now assert its own struc-

tural and mythical character against the full weight of the classical tradition. This particular "difference" is reinforced by the superimposition of a hinged column head, which, aside from serving as a metaphorical capital also inverts the position and significance of the welded steel hinged joint as this appeared in Peter Behrens's Turbinenfabrik of 1909. The hinges of the New National Gallery roof thus consolidate in their simple act of support the full tectonic heritage of Western building culture, while the egg-crate roof itself, painted a dark gray bordering on matte-black, depends for its reading on the ineffable play of planes of the same color, situated at different spatial depths, so that the intersecting lower flanges of the space-frame members seem to hover as a dark gray network below the planar continuity of an unspecified darkness and depth. Here Mies's "black-on-black," subject to the ever-changing impact of reflected light, answers, in the upper reaches of an egg-crate, to the persistent memory of the avant-garde. Thus we pass in one final heroic work from the technical and the tectonic resolution of a long-standing Neoclassical proposition, to the intangible, almost imperceptible, not to say mystical assertion of the sublime as this appeared in Malevich's white-on-white series of 1918.

Kenneth Frampton
October, 1984

1 Quoted in Werner Blaser, *Mies van der Rohe* (New York: Praeger, 1972), p. 10.
2 Mies van der Rohe, in "On Architectural Education," *Architectural Design*, March 1961.
3 Quoted in *Artnews*, September 1947, p. 21.
4 Quoted by Peter Carter in *Mies van der Rohe at Work* (New York: Praeger, 1974), p. 23.
5 Mies van der Rohe, in *Architectural Record*, September 1969.
6 Philip Johnson, *Mies van der Rohe* (New York: Museum of Modern Art, 1947), p. 35.
7 Wolf Tegethoff, *Mies van der Rohe. Die Villen und Landhausprojekte* (Essen: Richard Bacht, 1981).
8 See Peter Blake, interview with Mies van der Rohe, in *Four Great Makers of Modern Architecture*, typescript of symposium held at Columbia University School of Architecture, March–May 1961 (New York: Columbia University, 1963), p. 102.
9 Philip Johnson, *Mies van der Rohe* (New York: Museum of Modern Art, 1947).
10 Peter Blake, *The Master Builders* (New York: Norton, 1975), p. 221.

INTRODUCTION

*Beauty is the
splendor of Truth.*
St. Augustine

One of the most vivid memories from my childhood is riding along Chicago's Outer Drive late in August 1950. I was nearly nine years old, and my family and I were returning from our annual month-long visit with my grandparents who lived in northern Wisconsin. Traffic was heavy that afternoon. My father was frequently forced to drive at five miles per hour or less. Our slow progress was not irritating; it allowed lots of time to look at the sailboats dotting the lake and to study the tall buildings which formed a wall along the shore. Two buildings under construction were of particular interest to me that afternoon.

I cannot recall a time in my childhood when construction sites did not hold a special fascination; it seemed magical to me how various parts and pieces could be assembled to make a building. But my experience to date had been limited to small buildings—mainly houses—made of wood studs and joists, and covered with shingles, clapboard or brick. The two buildings under construction were made of steel. This alone was enough to attract and hold my attention.

Window frames were already installed on the lower floors of one of the towers. Columns and beams were being lifted into place near the top of the other tower. What made these two buildings different from their immediate neighbors (and from anything I had seen before) was that even as they were being enclosed, I could still see how they were constructed. With other buildings, once they were covered

in brick or wood, I could only guess what and where their structures were. . . Here, I could see their columns and beams through the windows . . . a floor-to-ceiling skin of glass which enclosed them. I felt just their clarity made them important; they "spoke" a language of architecture I did not then understand, but I could see it and feel it.

It was in 1959, nine years later, when I learned who had designed these buildings; it also happened to be the year that I decided to study architecture. As much by chance as by good fortune, I entered the school founded by the architect whose work had so impressed me as a child. Several months after I began my studies at the Illinois Institute of Technology, I passed by these same two skyscrapers as I was walking along the shore of Lake Michigan. They were the 860 and 880 Lake Shore Drive Apartments, buildings now so famous as the first all-glass skyscraper apartments that they are known only by their address. The intervening years had dulled neither their magic for me nor their attraction. They were as clear and as bold as I remembered and as wonderful.

Mies's approach to the *realization* of an architecture worthy of the name was carefully considered and rational. It presupposed that a synthesis could be achieved between science and technology, and between culture and aesthetics. It was an approach to architecture that was, at the same time, both simple and complex. It is significant to

1. Apartment building at 860 Lake Shore Drive, Chicago, Illinois, 1950. Installation of the curtain wall.

note that when speaking about his work or of architecture in general, he usually avoided such terms as "architecture" and "design" preferring instead "structure" and "*Baukunst.*"

By structure he meant a "complete morphological organism"[1] and not merely a set of beams, girders and columns. *Baukunst* held a clearer meaning for Mies than did architecture . . . "'*bau*' the construction and '*kunst*' just a refinement of that and nothing more."[2] It was characteristic of Mies van der Rohe to reduce everything to its clearest and most elemental form. While the clarity and integrity of his work attest to this, these qualities also offer the greatest obstacles to understanding and appreciating that work. Not only did Mies demand that we look at the

2. *View from Lake Michigan of Mies's four apartment buildings, 860, 880, 900, and 910 Lake Shore Drive, Chicago.*

work itself, he also demanded that we look beyond the work to its inner structure—to those ideas which reflect and animate an age.

Mies's work followed from history, but it did not imitate historical styles. It owed much to technology, but it was not, in itself, technology. When raised to the realm of art, it transcended structure, materials and technology to become the embodiment or spirit of its age—the *Zeitgeist.*

Mies explained his philosophy:

"I want things to be simple. Mind you: a simple person is not a simpleton. I like simplicity, probably because I like clarity, not because of cheapness or something like that. We never

think of reducing cost when we work.

Of course we also want to find new possibilities and search for them. But if there doesn't seem to be a really new way, we are not afraid to stick to the old; i.e., to what we have found out earlier. So you see, I don't design every building differently. Only if the task or the function demands it, then we work on new possibilities. Anyway, it is not new effects we are after.

I am interested in clear structure. Whether you do it with plasticine or what have you, I don't care. People say that concrete, because it is a plastic material, is a material that can be used for anything, but that isn't true. If you want clear structure, you must use concrete with clarity too. You know that it can also be used without clarity. But I don't do that. I want a structural architecture, because I believe that that is the only way by which we can have a communion with the essentials of our civilization."[3]

I began thinking about this book in 1977 when some students, who were about to graduate, asked me to talk with them about Mies. In 1974 I began to compile a bibliography, a chronology and an inventory of Mies's projects and completed works. This bibliography was published by Garland Publishing, Inc. (1979) as part of their Reference Series in the Humanities. Later, I taught a series of seminars devoted to the study of Mies's life and work. Teaching provided me with a forum in which those ideas were debated, refined and tested. As I began to understand Mies's work, I found in it a richness of content that appealed to the intellect as well as to the spirit.

The reader should note that the emphasis in chapters I, II and III focuses on those childhood and early adult experiences which, in combination, shaped Mies's architecture. However, in chapters IV and V there is a shift in emphasis to Mies's work itself. There are two reasons for this shift: first, when Mies immigrated to the United States in 1937, he was a mature and accomplished architect, and his work, after 1938, represents the continued realization and refinement of an established philosophy of architecture. Second, Mies was an intensely private person for whom his work was his life; Mies also believed that his work spoke as eloquently and with the clarity and forcefulness of the written word. He preferred to build, not to talk.

Although my experience and observations influenced the content and structure of this book, my intention was that these same observations and experience, serve as adjuncts to the commentaries of contemporary critics and historians as well as to Mies's written and spoken remarks. The end, to which my efforts and research have been directed, is the introduction of Mies's work to a new generation of students and scholars. I hope that this introduction will stimulate and facilitate a further examination of Mies's architecture for what it is rather than based on what others have believed it to be.

1 Peter Carter, "Mies van der Rohe, An Appreciation on the Occasion, This Month, of His 75th Birthday," *Architectural Design* 31 (March 1961): 96.
2 Ibid.
3 "Mies Speaks. 'I Do Not Design Buildings, I Develop Buildings,'" *Architectural Review* 144 (December 1968): 451.

CHAPTER I: 1886-1918

Reason is the first principle
of all human work.
—*St. Thomas Aquinas*

Until the advent of the Industrial Revolution, architectural history could have been written from the viewpoint that it consisted of the gradual development and refinement of different building types and structural systems. This process was evolutionary in nature since buildings grew out of and were a direct response to the available materials, the level of technological development, and the requirements and aspirations of a specific culture. In each culture, there existed a body of knowledge concerning the static and dynamic forces which determined a building's stability. This empirical knowledge had been arrived at through direct observation and experience over long periods. Some of the laws of mechanics and the strength of materials were understood; other results were arrived at through trial and error.

The Industrial Revolution changed not only how buildings were built but also why they were built. Factories and railway terminals in cast and wrought iron replaced stone temples and brick basilicas as dominant building types. Moreover, the mutual understanding of and appreciation for materials and technic, which previously existed among master builders and craftsmen, quickly gave way to new materials whose properties were only vaguely grasped by the emerging professions of engineering and architecture, much less by the laborers who replaced the craftsmen.

The rapid changes which industrialization and the new materials precipitated in the nineteenth century were felt at all levels of society; few individuals, however, understood this new capacity and fewer still appreciated the real potential of cast iron, reinforced concrete, glass and steel. With few exceptions architects in the nineteenth century were preoccupied with a seemingly endless progression of stylistic revivals, the ultimate effect of which was to impoverish the expressive value of architecture by exhausting its spirit and depriving it of meaning.

Ludwig Mies (van der Rohe was a later addition to his name) was born on March 27, 1886, in Aachen (Aix-la-Chapelle), Germany. He was the youngest of five children born to Michael Mies, a master mason and his wife Amalie. Despite the fact that his father owned and operated a stone cutting shop, the family was of humble origins; their lack of material means precluded an extensive education for any of the four children who survived childhood. Mies (as he was almost universally known during his professional life) described his education as follows:

"I had no conventional architectural education. I worked under a few good architects; I read a few good books—and that's about it." [1]

In actuality he attended Aachen's Cathedral School (Domschule) from the age six to thirteen. After school and during vacation, he acquired an education of a different kind, working for his father in the family's stone cutting

shop where he learned the physical properties of stone as a building material.

Of Amalie Mies little is known. Through her efforts and persistence, Mies attended Mass daily serving as a choirboy[2] in the chapel built by the Holy Roman Emperor, Charlemagne, nearly one thousand years earlier. At the beginning of the ninth century, Aachen, as the first capital of the Holy Roman Empire, had become the center of Western thought and civilization. Through Charlemagne's patronage and because of his influence, the city was endowed with a number of substantial buildings in addition to the chapel, his palace and a royal school. These Carolingian structures (along with others from later times) survived until World War I when many were destroyed.

Despite his mother's concern for his spiritual well-being, Mies was less interested in the transubstantiation of the Eucharist than he was in the way stones and mortar had been transformed into the structure and space in which the celebration took place. During Mass, he counted stones and traced mortar joints with his eyes.[3] From working in his father's stone cutting shop, he was able to follow the inner logic of the chapel's structure and the physical nature of the materials from which it was made. In trying to understand the way stones came together to form a wall, an arch or a vault, Mies was also attempting to "see" structure for what it would become for him later: an idea which ordered *all* the parts, a complete morphology.

The other buildings in Aachen also impressed him. Years after the departure from that city he recalled them (and his youth) with obvious feeling and sensitivity:

"I remember seeing many old buildings in my hometown when I was young. Few of them were important buildings. They were mostly very simple, but very clear. I was impressed by the strength of these buildings because they did not belong to any epoch. They had been there for over a thousand years and were still impressive, and nothing could change that. All the great styles passed, but they were still there. They didn't lose anything and they were still as good as on the day they were built. They were medieval buildings, not with any special character but they were really built.*"* [4]

The origin of Mies's interest in structure and architecture was the result of native ability combined with natural curiosity, the influence of his parents, and the impact of the built environment in which he lived.

In 1899 at thirteen, Mies left the Cathedral School and attended a local trade school (*Spenrathschule*) for two years. During this time he also worked as an apprentice brick mason for a local builder. Mies, like other apprentices, was not paid for his labors. Since both he and his family needed money, he went to work at the age of fifteen for a firm of interior decorators whose specialty was stucco decoration. Here he was able to employ his emerging talent for freehand drawing and to apply what he had already learned of basic construction skills. [5] Shortly after Mies's arrival, the firm's chief designer was conscripted into the Imperial German Army, and in recognition of his drawing talent, Mies was quickly promoted from "office boy" to "designer." Years later he recalled with obvious delight, but in mock horror, how mornings in the firm were spent drawing full-size cartoons for elaborate Louis XIV plaster ornaments for ceilings and walls; afternoons were spent designing more restrained Renaissance details. Soon he was able to draw even the most difficult and involved cartouches while looking in the opposite direction. He performed this feat frequently to the delight and dismay of his fellow employees. [6]

It was soon clear to Mies that designing stucco decorations was not developing his talents (except for drawing) or his intellect. The experience with the interior decorators had afforded him the opportunity of seeing the work of local architects and working closely with a few of them. In 1904, after three years with the firm, Mies took a job in an architect's office and began to learn the skills expected of an architect. He was assigned to one of the available worktables in the drafting room; as he was putting his drafting instruments in one of the table's drawers, he discovered a copy of a scientific paper left by a previous draftsman. In the paper were described the various physi-

21

6. *Riehl house, Berlin-Neubabelsberg, Germany, 1907.*

7. *Riehl house. View from the lower garden.*

cal aspects of the structure of the universe. This chance event ignited in Mies an interest in science—especially astrophysics—which he retained for the rest of his life. After philosophy, his other great intellectual passion, Mies's reading focused on the sciences.[7]

Following a year's office experience, Mies decided to move to Berlin where several prominent architects had their offices. As the capital of the German empire, Berlin offered more opportunities for professional development and advancement than did Aachen. Because Mies had a limited working knowledge of wood as a material for architecture, he sought employment in the office of an architect/designer known for his appreciation of this material and for his sensitive use of it, Bruno Paul (1874–1968). For Mies the choice of this office was fortuitous: not only did working for Paul expose him to the merits and limitations of wood used for structure and in furniture, but, under Paul's tutelage, those abiding qualities of Mies's work—his sensitivity to materials, to structure and to proportions—began to take recognizable form and expression.

Mies left Paul's office in 1907 after two years there. His departure was precipitated by the fact that he had just received the commission for a modest private residence, which was to be his first independent work. The work for *Geheimrat* (privy councillor) Prof. Dr. Riehl, a professor of philosophy, and his family was in the neighborhood's prevailing tradition of domestic architecture. It was a simple mass with a pitched roof. However, what distinguished it from its neighbors was the way Mies sited the house to take advantage of the slope and his evident concern for proportions and details. By using the same motif for the doors and panelling of the dining room, he gave a quiet, unexpected elegance to this modest space. Similar and equally sensitive refinements were in evidence throughout the house. As one critic wrote shortly after the house was completed: "The work is so faultless that no one would guess it is the first independent work of a young architect."[8]

The Riehl house established Mies as an architect of quality, sensitivity and promise. As far as he was concerned, there

22

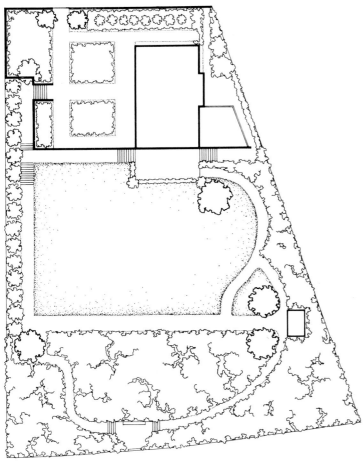

8. Riehl house. Site plan.

9. Riehl house. First and second floor plans.

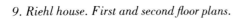

10, 11. Riehl house. Exterior and interior views.

12, 13. Riehl house. Interior views.

remained only one impediment to his further success—his surname.[9] In German "mies" translates as "out of sorts, poor, bad or wretched." It would not do for Mies to have his professional accomplishments linked to (or hindered by) a surname which carried with it the connotation of wretchedness. So in "the fashion of ambitious young professionals of the day,"[10] he attached the noble "van der Rohe," a variation of his mother's maiden name.

Despite this somewhat pretentious gesture, he was always known as Mies to friends and associates. No one ever called him Ludwig except the immediate members of his family. He was addressed as Ludwig Mies van der Rohe only on the most formal of occasions and by people who did not know him. Later, when the quality of his work was universally recognized, "mies," ironically enough, came to be accepted as a synonym for precision, refinement and elegance.

While in Berlin, Mies was exposed to the work of two individuals whose influence helped shape his own ideas about architecture: Karl Friedrich Schinkel (1781–1841) and Peter Behrens (1868–1940). During the nineteenth century, Schinkel was Gemany's leading neo-classical architect. His influence extended well beyond his death, certainly up to the end of the century.

Mies found Schinkel's carefully proportioned buildings, his sensitive use of materials, and his expressive details appealing and instructive. It was, however, Schinkel's attitude toward the then emergent industrial age which most influenced Mies. Schinkel believed that this new age should develop an appropriate architectural expression free of historical influence.[11] Schinkel's own *Bauakademie* in Berlin intimates what he had in mind. He expressed the building's structure and spatial organization on its exterior with clarity and economy of means. The result was handsome in its own right and relatively free of historical references and surface decoration.

Mies came under Peter Behrens's direct influence after two years of independent practice when, in 1908, he joined Behrens's office. As a leading member of the late *Schinkel-*

schule (followers or students of Schinkel), Behrens became, on his appointment as "artistic advisor" to the AEG (*Allgemeine Elektricitäts-Gesellschaft*, the German equivalent of the General Electric Company), one of the most important and influential architects in Europe at this time.

Many other talented architects were also drawn to Behrens's office including Walter Gropius (1883–1969) who worked for Behrens as his assistant from late in 1907 to 1910 and who would later found the *Bauhaus*.[12] For five months during 1910, Charles-Edouard Jeanneret (1887–1965), later known professionally as Le Corbusier, also worked in Behrens's office. So for a brief period three of the future leaders of the Modern Movement in architecture were employed by the individual whose work, according to the philosophy of the German *Werkbund*,[13] represented the ideal collaboration between artist and industry.

The *Werkbund* was founded late in 1907. About one hundred of Germany's leading industrialists, artists and art lovers met in Munich to re-establish the essential links between art and industry . . . between craft and mass production.[14] Their goal was to inject the aesthetic element into German economic life thereby making German manufactured goods more appealing and more competitive in the world market.

While the *Werkbund's* membership deplored the destruction of artistic sensibilities and craftsmanship associated with the pre-industrial past, they accepted the fact that the progress of industrialization and mass production were irresistible.[15] Their approach was to counter the excessive materialism and rationalism, the negative by-products of the Industrial Revolution, by designed example and through a rigorous program of education. This was to be accomplished without sacrificing the potential for higher quality manufactured goods at more competitive prices.

During the three years Mies worked for Behrens, first under Gropius and later as Behrens's assistant, the office was responsible for the design of letterheads, light fixtures, and a Turbine Factory in Berlin (1908), all for the AEG, as

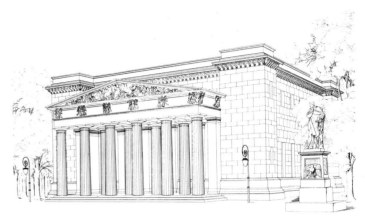
14. Neue Wache, Berlin, Germany. Karl Friedrich Schinkel, 1816–18.

15. Altes Museum, Berlin, Germany. Karl Friedrich Schinkel, 1822–30.

25

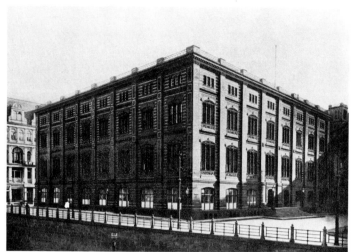

16. Bauakademie, Berlin, Germany. Karl Friedrich Schinkel, 1831–36.

17. Bauakademie. Entrance.

well as the German Embassy in St. Petersburg, Russia (1911–12). Gropius left the office in 1910 and established his own practice. Mies's experience and ability made him the logical choice to succeed Gropius. As Behrens's assistant, Mies supervised the construction of the embassy and made numerous trips to what was then the Russian capital.[16]

In 1911, while still a member of the office, Mies designed a residence for Hugo Perls in a suburb of Berlin. The house is a solid, almost severe, building in the still prevalent tradition of Schinkel. Its stuccoed walls were unornamented: its simplicity was enhanced by the proportions and placement of the openings. However, as influential as Schinkel's work was on Mies, the Perls house represents the work of a confident and mature architect who had incorporated the spirit and principles of Schinkel's work into his own approach to architecture.[17]

Meanwhile as Behrens's assistant, Mies worked on a design for a large museum-like residence for Mme. H.E.L.J. Kröller, owner of the famous Kröller-Müller collection of paintings. Behrens's solution, a full-size model of which was constructed from wood and canvas on the site, was rejected for a variety of reasons. It was an ungainly structure, neo-classical in spirit. Its massing was awkward and lacked the formal integrity found in Schinkel's work. (Behrens seemed less sure of himself in his residential work than as the AEG's artistic advisor. His designs for the AEG, especially the factories, were simply massed with clear structures and enclosed in a straightforward, rational manner.)

Mme. Kröller was, however, impressed with Mies, and she and her husband invited him to The Hague to prepare his own design for their residence. As Mies described it:

"I was taken round Holland for a couple of weeks so that I should get to know the country. I knew it from just across the frontier from Aachen. And then, one fine day, Mrs. Kröller said to me she had thought it over with her husband, and wouldn't I like to produce the design."[18]

The offer of this commission came as Mies and Behrens were experiencing difficulties in their professional rela-

18. German Embassy, St. Petersburg, Russia. Peter Behrens,
1911–12. Entrance.

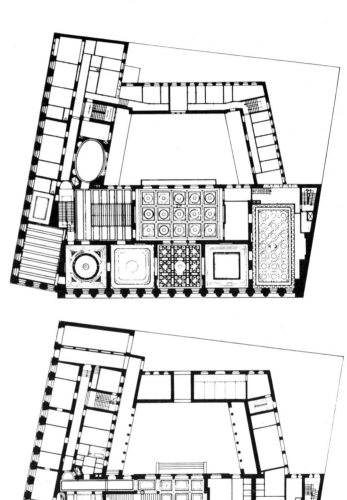

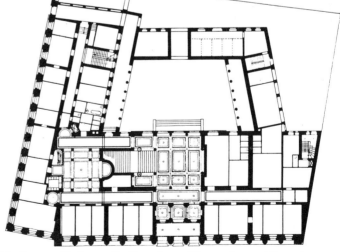

19. German Embassy, St. Petersburg. First and second floor plans.

20. *Perls house, Berlin-Zehlendorf, Germany, 1911.*

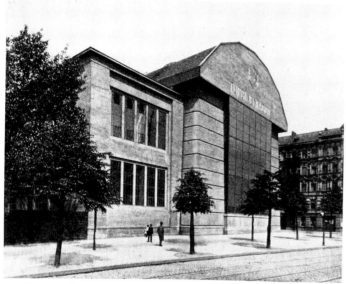

21. *Turbine Factory, Berlin, Germany. Peter Behrens, 1909.*

tionship. Disagreements had arisen over the management of the construction of the embassy in St. Petersburg. In addition Behrens was angered by the fact that Mies had been able to keep the construction costs within the budget, whereas he had been unsuccessful in his attempts to accomplish this.[19]

During the year he lived at The Hague, Mies had a studio in the Kröllers' home. The walls were hung with paintings from their extensive collection—especially van Gogh's paintings. Through this exposure Mies developed his appreciation for art in general and a discerning eye for van Gogh's work.[20]

Mies's design was also constructed in wood and canvas on the actual site. And like Behrens's, it too was rejected. However, the year spent with the Kröllers was hardly wasted; for in addition to working on plans for their residence, Mies entered the competition for a Bismarck Memorial at Bingen-on-the-Rhine, Germany (1912). Both the Kröller house and the memorial project manifested the strength and clarity of Schinkel's work. Mies did not hesitate to break with his Prussian master; in the grouping of the second story windows of the Kröller house, the continuous horizontal window band, rather than a series of isolated openings, anticipates the fenestration of his later Concrete Country House project (1924). The long elevation of the Bismarck Memorial reads more like a series of overlapping solids (or planes) in space, a device which is similar in many respects to the relationships of the brick masses in his monument to Karl Liebknecht and Rosa Luxemburg in Berlin (1926).

Aside from Schinkel, Mies often credited the modern pioneers to whom he felt indebted. From Behrens, Mies said, he "learned great form"; from Berlage[21] he "learned great structure." But the individual whose influence on Mies was more subtle, less literal—yet more profound than either Behrens's or Berlage's—was Frank Lloyd Wright (1867–1959) whom Mies was not to meet until 1937. Mies was first made aware of Wright in 1910 when a major exhibition of his work was mounted in Berlin. This exhibi-

22. *Kröller residence, The Hague, The Netherlands. Peter Behrens, 1911. Exterior perspective.*

23. *Bismarck Monument entitled "Germany's Gratitude," 1910. Elisenhöhe, near Bingerbrück-Bingen, Germany. Perspective. Illustration 77, with caption "Deutschlands Dank Architekten E. und L. Mies—Aachen," from the book* Bismark-National-Denkmal Hundert Wettbewerb Entwürfe *by Max Schmid, Düsseldorf, 1911.*

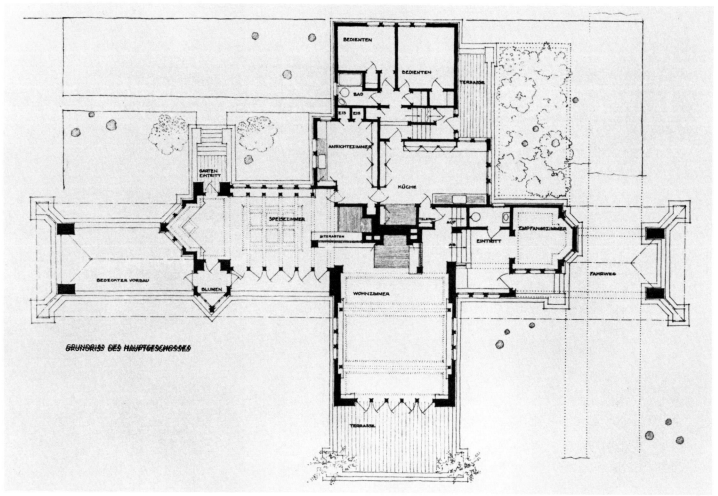

24. *Ward W. Willits house, Highland Park, Illinois. Frank Lloyd Wright, 1901–02. First floor plan.*

tion coincided with the publication of a portfolio of Wright's drawings by the famous Wasmuth publishing house in Berlin.

But Wright's influence on Mies began to manifest itself only after World War I, especially in Mies's project for the Brick Country House (1923). Here Mies consciously relates spaces to each other by having them flow into one another and by breaking down the distinction between interior and exterior spaces. For Wright a building was not a collection of box-like rooms but a total, integrated spatial experience punctuated and articulated by walls and planes.

Thirty years later in 1940 for an unpublished exhibition catalogue, Mies described the impact Wright's work had after the turn of the century on many European architects, including himself:

"The work of this great master presented an architectural world of unexpected force, clarity of language and disconcerting richness of form. Here, finally, was a master-builder drawing upon the veritable fountainhead of architecture; who with true originality lifted his creations into the light. Here again, at long last, genuine architecture flowered. The more we were absorbed in the study of these creations, the

30

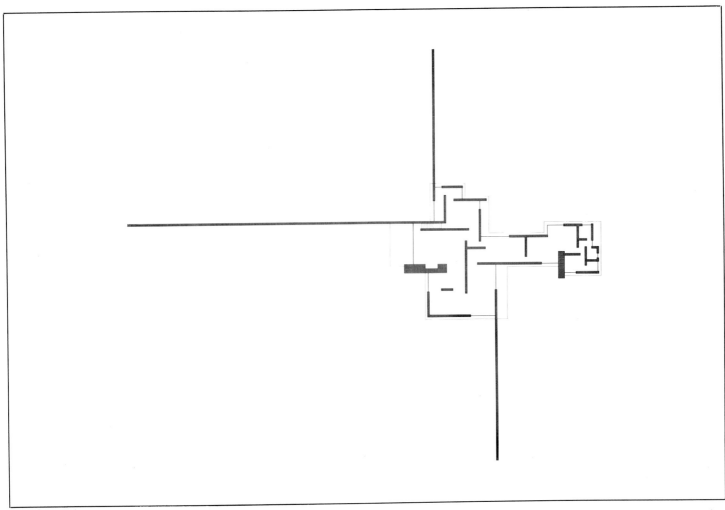

25. *Brick Country House, 1923. Plan.*

greater became our admiration for his incomparable talent, the boldness of his conceptions and the independence of his thought and action. The dynamic impulse emanating from his work invigorated a whole generation. His influence was strongly felt even when it was not actually visible."[22]

In 1913 Mies returned to Berlin from The Hague and re-established himself as an independent architect. On his return he designed the Urbig residence which, built in 1914, was in the tradition of an eighteenth-century villa. This work demonstrated Mies's assimilation of Schinkel's principles; it also presages his rejection of Schinkel's

neo-classicism. Aware of the change which had taken place, Mies, during an interview in 1968, recounted an exchange between Behrens and himself shortly after his return from The Hague:

"Berlage's Exchange (at Amsterdam) had impressed me enormously. Behrens was of the opinion that it was all passé, but I said to him: "Well, if you aren't badly mistaken." He was furious; he looked as if he wanted to hit me. What interested me most in Berlage was his careful construction, honest to the bones. And his spiritual attitude had nothing to do with classicism, nothing with historic styles

31

26. Stock Exchange, Amsterdam. The Netherlands. Hendrik Petrus Berlage, 1909.

altogether. After Berlage I had to fight with myself to get away from the classicism of Schinkel."[23]

Germany mobilized for war, and shortly after the Urbig house was completed, Mies was called up for active duty. The lack of a university education prevented him from serving in the army as an officer. As an enlisted man, he supervised construction of roads and concrete bridges in Rumania and the Balkans from 1914 to 1918.[24]

The pragmatic nature of the war as well as its architecture, plus his exposure to Berlage's work, finally freed Mies from the stylistic preoccupations and traditions of nineteenth-century architecture. Nowhere was the unloading of this aesthetic baggage more clearly demonstrated than in the sketches he did for his own house in Werder (1914). It was to have been an eighteenth-century villa set amid an ordered, formal landscape. In its massing and its relationship to the landscape, the house was rooted in a former time, a veritable symbol of the "old order." He did one last design, a project for the Kempner residence (1919). The stage was set for him to take a new approach to architecture—an approach predicated on new materials, new ideas about structure, and new ideas about space.

1 Katherine Kuh, "Mies van der Rohe: Modern Classicist," *Saturday Review* 48 (January 23, 1965): 61.
2 Personal communication with Georgia van der Rohe, Mies's daughter.
3 Peter Carter, "Mies van der Rohe, An Appreciation on the Occasion, This Month, of His 75th Birthday," *Architectural Design* 31 (March 1961): 97.
4 Ibid.
5 According to Georgia van der Rohe, "Mies was not the only member of his family with design talent. His older brother, Ewald, was a designer of some distinction of tombstones and funeral monuments."
6 "Mies Speaks. 'I Do Not Design Buildings, I Develop Buildings,'" *Architectural Review* 144 (December 1968): 451.
7 Personal communication with Georgia van der Rohe.
8 "Architekt Ludwig Mies: Villa Des . . . Prof. Dr. Riehl in Neubabelsberg," *Moderne Bauformen* 9 (1910): 42–48.
9 Personal communication with Georgia van der Rohe.
10 Franz Schulz, *Mies van der Rohe: Interior Spaces* (Chicago: The Arts Club of Chicago, 1982), 6.
11 Karl Friedrich Schinkel, *Aus Schinkel's Nachlass: Reisetagebücher, Briefe und Aphorismen, mitgetheilt und mit einem Verzeichniss sämmtlicher Werk Schinkel's versehen, von Alfred Freiherrn von Wolzogen* (Berlin: Verlag der Königlichen geheimen ober-hofbuch druckerei [R. Decker] 1862–64), 208.
12 There exists no good literal translation for the term *Bauhaus*. While the *Bauhaus* existed as a physical place, a school, it was also an idea. It was an

27. Urbig house, Berlin-Neubabelsberg, Germany, 1914.

28. A house for the architect, Werder, Germany, 1914.

idea about education (and about life) and the relationship of that education to art, craft and technology.

13 Like the term *Bauhaus*, no simple literal translation exists for *Werkbund*. It is a compound word, a compound idea. At one level it was an organization to promote a closer relationship between artists and industry, between what is produced and the quality of that production. As we shall see, it was also an idea about the quality of life and the role manufactured goods play in the determination of that quality.

14 Joan Campbell, *The German Werkbund: The Politics of Reform in the Applied Arts* (Princeton: Princeton University Press, 1978), 9.

15 Ibid., 10–11.

16 Alan Windsor, *Peter Behrens, Architect and Designer* (New York: Whitney Library of Design, Watson-Guptill Publications, 1981), 123.

17 As André Gide observed: "Influence creates nothing. It awakens."

18 "Mies Speaks.," *Architectural Review*, 451.

19 Windsor, *Peter Behrens, Architect and Designer*, 123.

20 "Mies Speaks.," *Architectural Review*, 451.

21 Like Behrens, Hendrik Peter Berlage's (1865–1934) influence extended beyond architecture and embraced all aspects of design. His talent dominated aesthetic life at the turn of the century in the Netherlands. And it was he who was finally awarded the commission for the Kröller residence.

22 Philip Johnson, *Mies van der Rohe* (New York: Museum of Modern Art, 1953), 201.

23 "Mies Speaks.," *Architectural Review*, 451.

24 Personal communication with Georgia van der Rohe.

33

29. *Office Building, Friedrichstrasse, Berlin, Germany, 1919. Collage.*

CHAPTER II: 1919-1926

It may well be that what we have hitherto understood as architecture, and what we are beginning to understand of technology are incompatible disciplines. The architect who proposes to run with technology knows now that he will be in fast company, and that, in order to keep up, he may have to emulate the Futurists and discard his whole cultural load, including the professional garments by which he is recognized as an architect.[1]
—*Reyner Banham, 1960.*

Mies emerged from the war without the cynicism or despair which marked so many other veterans. Like other creative individuals, Mies felt liberated by the abdication of the Kaiser and the defeat of the old order. He was profoundly stimulated by the promise of the Weimar Republic. While his work prior to World War I was essentially traditional in style and in its use of materials, nothing about it anticipates the creativity and originality which marked his work during the five years after the armistice. Between 1919 and 1924, he produced five seminal projects which expanded the limits of their respective materials: the two Glass Skyscrapers (1919–1921), the Concrete Office Building (1922), the Brick Country House (1923) and the Concrete Country House (1924). They clearly demonstrated the spatial and structural potential of the materials associated with modern architecture—glass, steel and reinforced concrete.

Each project was unique in conception, definition and expression. In their originality and sensitivity to line, texture and value, Mies's drawings are like the buildings they represent. No disparity exists between the *idea* of the building and the *technique* used to represent it. The idea which unifies these projects derives from the thesis that is fundamental to understanding Mies's architecture: that technology is the most significant force animating architecture and society in the twentieth century. It is, to quote Mies's famous phrase, the "will of the epoch."[2]

Four of these five seminal projects were first seen at a series of annual exhibitions sponsored by the *Novembergruppe* (November group),[3] so named for the month of the Republican Revolution in Germany. The *Novembergruppe* from its inception in 1918 until the 1930's had as its stated purpose the promotion of modern art in the most general sense. It formed the core of the Modern Movement in Germany. The exposure and acclaim Mies received through these exhibitions was such that he came to be thought of as "an architect's architect"[4] by other members of the European community of architects.

In addition to the *Novembergruppe*, other organizations were formed after World War I to overcome official resistance or prejudice to the Modern Movement. Those to the left of the *Werkbund* advocated an activist approach. The more radical groups were less concerned with Germany's post-war economic health than were the members of the *Werkbund*. The radicals viewed architecture as the most social of the arts and, therefore, the most political. Through architecture they hoped to bring about social change and realize a new social order.

In the often heady and volatile years after the war, it appeared to some that architecture and not the *Werkbund's* moderate position was the way to change society.[5] It was, however, contrary to Mies's nature for architects to have their work (including his own) politicized. He cared not

35

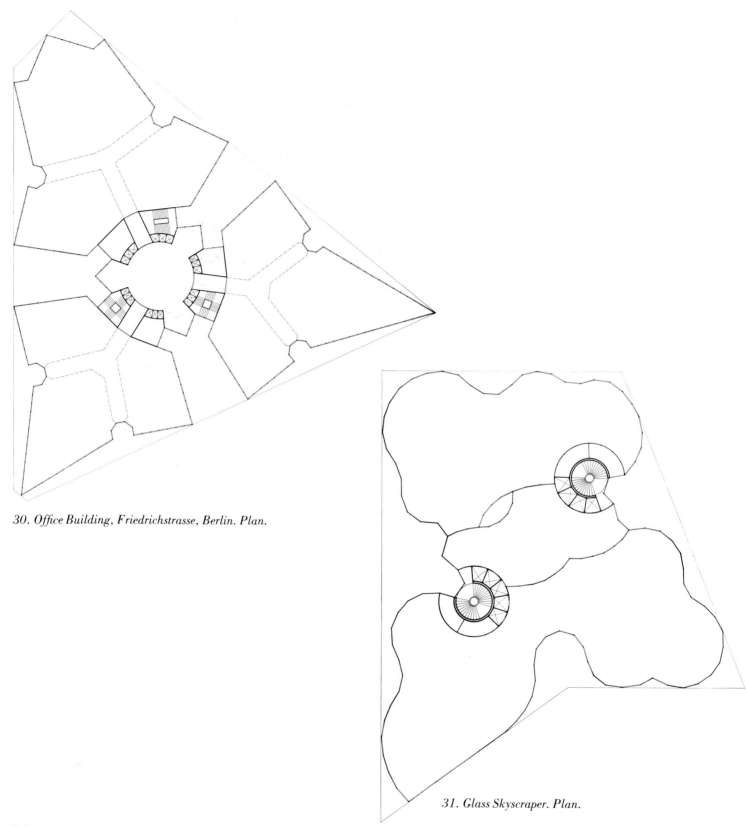

30. Office Building, Friedrichstrasse, Berlin. Plan.

31. Glass Skyscraper. Plan.

36

32. Glass Skyscraper. Model.

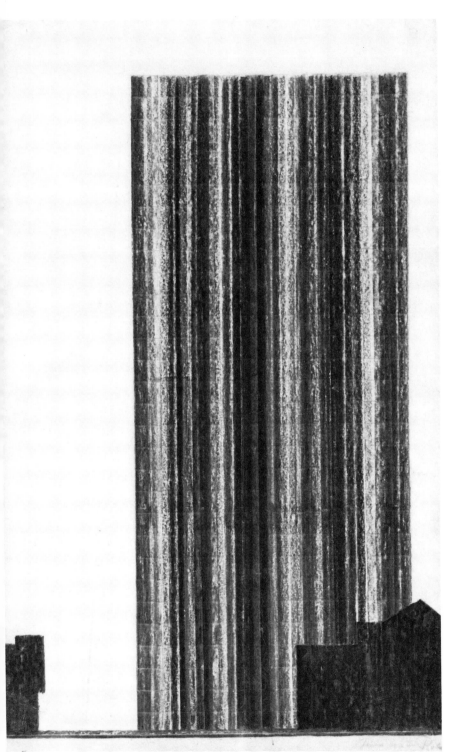

33. *Glass Skyscraper. Charcoal and conte crayon elevation.*

what an individual's politics were but how good the work was: what interested him was the work's quality and integrity.

As the decade progressed, Mies became involved with a number of organizations which supported the Modern Movement. Through them he used a variety of ways to present the case for modern art and architecture to the general public. As a member of the *Novembergruppe*, he directed its annual exhibition from 1921 to 1925. Late in 1923, he and Hans Richter, a de Stijl abstractionist and film maker, published the magazine *G* (for *Gestaltung*— creative force or action). *G* was devoted to contemporary artistic movements (Dada, the Constructivists, as well as de Stijl) and scientific developments as they related to or influenced technology. In 1925 he helped found the *Zehner Ring* (Ring of Ten)[6] whose purpose, like that of the *Novembergruppe*, was the promotion of the Modern Movement. And from 1926 to 1932, as first vice president of the *Werkbund*, he directed two important exhibitions dedicated to the new architecture (*neues bauen* as it was called) in Stuttgart (1927) and Berlin (1931).

Mies's involvement with these organizations provided the means for artistic, not political, expression. Mies remained politically reticent throughout his life. He avoided polemics, preferring reason, logic and a solid body of work as the means by which individuals and governments might come to understand the validity and necessity for modern architecture. For Mies architecture was a function of industrialization and new materials, of structure and space. It had to be accepted and understood on its own terms free from political implications or associations. As he wrote in 1924:

"Architecture is the will of an epoch translated into space. Until this simple truth is clearly recognized, the new architecture will be uncertain and tentative. Until then it must remain a chaos of undirected forces. The question as to the nature of architecture is of decisive importance. It must be understood that all architecture is bound up with its own time, that it can only be manifested in living tasks and in the medium of its epoch. In no age has it been otherwise." [7]

Given such a statement, it would be most tempting to accept the position generally held by critics and historians that Mies's work immediately following the end of World War I, was directly influenced by two contemporary artistic movements: de Stijl and German Expressionism. However, such a position formulated in retrospect appears based only on superficial similarities between Mies's work and the aesthetics of these two movements and not on shared attitudes or a similar philosophy.

As a group the Expressionists were motivated to express their feelings through art. Such an approach is inherently subjective rather than objective, lacking a consistent, commonly shared vocabulary for expression. As early as 1922, Mies affirmed that his approach to architecture was

directly influenced by the physical and structural properties of the materials he used. Describing his Glass Skyscrapers, he wrote that these two projects were predicated on considerations of function, material, structure and *not* on expression for its own sake. [8]

In later life he explained what his concerns were at this time:

"Because I was using glass, I was anxious to avoid enormous, dead surfaces reflecting too much light, so I broke the facades a little in plan so that light should fall on them at different angles: like crystal, cut-crystal. That was for a competition—it was exhibited in Berlin in the Old Town Hall. They pushed my design into a dark corner, probably because they thought it was a joke. Then I tried to work with smaller areas of glass and adjusted my strips of glass to the light and then pushed them into a (flat horizontal) plasticine plane. That gave me the curve, and if people now say that I got that from Arp, I can tell you it had nothing to do with him. I had no Expressionist intention, I wanted to show the skeleton, and I thought that the best way would be simply to put a glass skin on." [9]

As the founder and spiritual force behind de Stijl, Theo van Doesburg (1884–1931) formulated a "universal" theory of art as he attempted to include artists, sculptors, designers and architects within the membership. Like Expressionism, de Stijl remained essentially an artistic move-

34. *Brick Country House, 1923. Exterior perspective.*

35. *Concrete Office Building, 1922. Exterior perspective.*

40

ment—few buildings were constructed. Within a few years, the architects who first embraced de Stijl found its purist vocabulary too limiting and abandoned it.

Mies was philosophically removed and detached from both groups. He could not accept expression for its own sake, nor could he accept an approach to architecture—no matter how universal its appeal—which was not based primarily on material and functional concerns. In one of the issues of *G* (1923), he articulated his position clearly and succinctly without philosophic cant: "Essentially our task is to free the practice of building from the control of aesthetic speculators and restore it to what it should exclusively be: building."[10]

During the incredibly inflationary period which wracked Germany's post-war economy, it was not Mies's philosophic position nor his objections to "aesthetic speculators" which prevented him from building; it was the state of the economy. From the end of the war until 1924, he built only three residences: the Kempner house, Berlin (1921); the Mosler house, Berlin-Neubabelsberg (1924); and the Wolf house, Guben (1924–26). During the same period he also designed some blocks of municipal apartments on the Afrikanischestrasse, Berlin (1925–26), and the monument to Karl Liebknecht and Rosa Luxembourg, the communist leaders who were murdered in 1919 (1926). Of these, none approaches either the spatial richness or structural daring

articulated in the five earlier projects. Only the monument with its projecting planes of rough brickwork suggests the architectural possibilities of a series of solids and planes in space.

With the exception of the Afrikanischestrasse apartments, the exterior surfaces of Mies's brick buildings from this time were unrendered. Their exposed, carefully bonded walls revealed their brick construction and their function as bearing walls. Even the rendered surfaces of the apartment buildings expressed their load-bearing function through the sensitive placement and proportions of the door and window openings. By such simple means, Mies distinguished himself from the proponents of de Stijl for whom materials were "dematerialized" and treated as abstract surfaces, subordinated to aesthetic ends, and without structural expression.

Controversy and misunderstanding still surround Mies's acceptance of a commission for a monument commemorating the assassinated communist leaders.[11] Accepting this commission was no more a political act than was his entry into the competition for a memorial to Bismarck or the conversion of Schinkel's *Neue Wache* (new guard-house) in Berlin to a memorial (1930) to the dead of World War I. Mies saw them only as design problems. Were it not for the addition of a hammer and sickle, the rough wall could be a memorial to anyone or anything. It was a sculptural, politi-

41

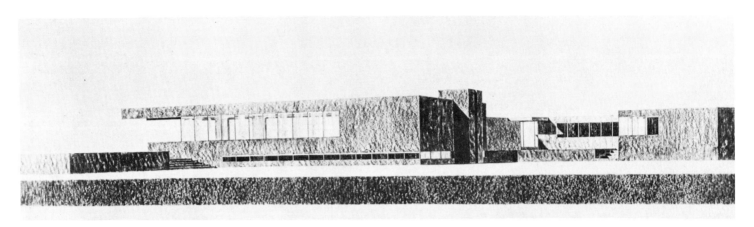

36, 37. Concrete Country House, 1924. Perspective and model.

38. Memorial to the World War I dead, Berlin, Germany, 1930. Interior perspective.

cally neutral surface.

If anything, designing the Liebknecht and Luxemburg monument was an act of accommodation for a client, Dr. Edward Fuchs. Fuchs, a prominent art collector and member of the German Communist Party, purchased the Perls house and wished to have it enlarged by the architect. During the course of his conversations with Mies regarding the proposed addition, Fuchs asked Mies if he would comment on a design for the monument proposed by another architect. Mies did, and after some time he observed that the movement's neo-classical design would be expensive to construct and appeared antithetic to the two communists' beliefs. Fuchs agreed.[12] So Mies designed a thick wall and constructed it of bricks which had been fired too long or at too high a temperature. Because these bricks were rough and irregular, they cost nothing—only the effort of carting them away.

As he approached his fortieth birthday, Mies's reputation for building with sensitivity and precision was recognized and clearly established. And having assimilated the ideas and the principles of his acknowledged masters, he stood at the threshold of a new and important stage in his career. While the magnitude of his talent had yet to be realized, behind him lay a significant body of seminal projects and completed works.

As encouraging as the future looked in 1926, what Mies had achieved since the end of the war had not been without its price. He was not particularly well-suited to family life because work took precedence over everyone and everything else. He needed quiet and solitude in which to think and work. In a family with three small children, quiet and solitude are rare. So in 1925, Mies's wife Ada, neé Bruhn (1885–1951), the daughter of a well-to-do Berlin industrialist whom he had married in 1914, decided that she and their three daughters should live apart from Mies. It was to remain a physical and not a legal separation, for neither party ever sought a divorce.[13]

1 Reyner Banham, *Theory and Design in the First Machine Age* (London: Architectural Press, 1960), 329–30.
2 Ludwig Mies van der Rohe, "Baukunst und Zeitwille," *Der Querschnitt* 4 (1924): 31–32.
3 Max Pechstein, César Klein, Georg Tappert, Heinrich Richter and Moritz Melzer were the *Novembergruppe*'s original founders. Shortly thereafter the five were joined by Karl Jacob Hirsch, Bernhard Hasler, Richard Janthur, Rudolf Bauer, Bruno Krauskopf, Otto Freundlich, Wilhelm Schmid, Rudolf Belling and Erich Mendelsohn. In all, according to historian Helga Kliemann, over 150 artists (in the broadest sense of that word), lovers of art and architects were affiliated in one way or another with the *Novembergruppe* during its existence. Among them were Hans Arp, Peter Behrens, Hendrik Petrus Berlage, Theo van Doesburg, Viking Eggeling, Lyonel Feininger, George Grosz, Walter Gropius, Hugo Häring, Ludwig Hilberseimer, Johannes Itten, Wassily Kandinsky, Gyorgy Kepes, Paul Klee, Arthur Korn, El Lissitzky, Hans and Wassily Luckhardt, Laszlo Moholy-Nagy, Georg Muche, Jacobus Johannes Pieter Oud, Hans Poelzig, Adolf Rading, Hans Richter, Oskar Schlemmer, Georg Scholz, Arthur Segal, Mart Stam, Bruno and Max Taut, Heinrich Tessenow, and Mies. For the complete list, see: Helga Kliemann, *Die Novembergruppe* (Berlin: Mann Verlag, 1969), 92–136.
4 Personal communication with Howard Dearstyne, an American student at the Bauhaus.
5 Contrary to what its critics charged, the *Werkbund*'s impact extended beyond improving the design of utilitarian objects. The *Werkbund* raised the design consciousness of all those who cared to look at or listen to what the *Werkbund* presented.
6 In addition to Mies, members of the *Zehner Ring* were: Otto Bartning, W. C. Behrendt, Peter Behrens, Richard Döcker, Walter Gropius, Hugo Häring, Haesler-Celle, Ludwig Hilberseimer, Arthur Korn, Karl Krayl, Hans Luckhardt, Wassily Luckhardt, Ernst May, Erich Mendelsohn, Adolf Meyer, Bernhard Pankok, Hans Poelzig, Adolf Rading, Hans Soeder, Hans Scharoun, Walter Schilbach, Karl Schneider, Bruno Taut, Max Taut, Heinrich Tessenow, and Martin Wagner.
7 Mies van der Rohe, "Baukunst und Zeitwille," 31–32.
8 Ludwig Mies van der Rohe, "Hochhausprojekt für Bahnhof Friedrichstrasse in Berlin," *Fruhlicht* 1 (1922): 122–24.
9 "Mies Speaks.," *Architectural Review*, 451.
10 MVDR [Mies van der Rohe], "Bauen," *G* (Berlin), no. 2 (September 1923): 1.
11 According to historian John Willett, thirty other communists who were also murdered are buried at the Liebknecht-Luxemburg memorial. See John Willett, *Art and Politics in the Weimar Period* (New York: Pantheon, 1978), 132.
12 Personal communication with Dirk Lohan, Mies's grandson.
13 Personal communication with Georgia van der Rohe.

39. Monument to Karl Liebknecht and Rosa Luxemburg, Berlin, Germany, 1926.

Page 46
40. Ionic Column and Mies's column for the New National Gallery, Berlin, 1962–68.

CHAPTER III: 1927-1937

*As I got up to leave I noticed a beautiful
engraving of an Ionic capital, prominent in
the modern room and asked what it was
doing there. Miës looked at it seriously for
a moment before replying. "The old architects," he said finally, "copy this sort of
thing. We appreciate it."* [1]
—*George Nelson, 1935*

During the mid-1920s, whether of necessity or by inclina-
tion, Mies focused his attention on the functional, technical and aesthetic problems associated with the design of
furniture. "Mies's crafts background and personal inclina-
tions," according to Ludwig Glaeser, "made him at first
follow the traditional approach and treat the interiors of his
early houses as parts of the entire architectural scheme." [2]
In this respect, his approach was not unlike Wright's, for
Wright, too, viewed the interiors of his buildings as part of
a larger architectural whole. As a result, Mies designed
furniture for specific locations in specific interiors and had
it produced in limited quantities. [3]

A side chair Mies designed for his own apartment reflects
his attitude toward furniture at this time (ca. 1926) as well
as his experience in the offices of Bruno Paul and Peter
Behrens. Nothing about it anticipates the metal furniture
for which he became world famous. The chair's wood frame
was veneered in rosewood; its seat and back were covered
with parchment. Its elegant proportions and careful refinement distinguish it from the work of his contemporaries.
Mies was not content, however, to refine details and proportions of existing furniture, nor did he wish to be necessarily limited to traditional materials or construction. The
debate of wood versus metal for furniture carried on by
others did not interest him at all. [4] His attitude was that
each material had its appropriate use and expression; one

material was not inherently better than another. "We must
remember," he wrote, "that everything depends upon how
we use a material, not on the material itself." [5]

Early in 1927 Mies began experimenting with the use of
bent steel tubing as the primary structural element for the
first MR (for *M*ies van der *R*ohe) furniture, a side
chair. Earlier attempts by others—a chaise longue (1904)
and a chair by Nolan (1922)—used frames of steel bars
formed into a coil which exploited the resultant spring
for resilience. Marcel Breuer (1902–81) and Mart Stam
(1899–   ) produced tubular steel furniture in 1925 and
1926 respectively. But Breuer's chair was rigid. And
Stam's used the principle of the cantilever unsuccessfully:
despite the fact that the curved portions of the tubular steel
frames were reinforced through the insertion of solid steel
bars, Stam's chairs sagged. [6] The MR chairs were the first
to have "exploited consistently the spring quality of steel
tubes." [7] Mies succeeded where others had failed not because of previous experience with steel tubing or the
method of its fabrication, but because he recognized the
potential of an idea *and* pursued it patiently to its ultimate
technical and aesthetic refinement. [8]

Concurrent with his work on the MR chair and as a direct
result of his position as first vice president of the *Werkbund*, Mies was awarded three commissions in 1927: the
most important was his appointment as director of the

47

41. *Rosewood and parchment side chair, ca. 1926. Mies designed a set of these chairs for his apartment in Berlin.*

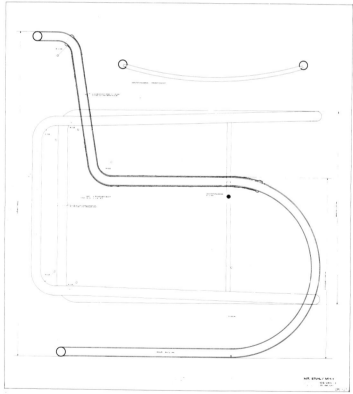

42. *MR chair, 1926. Plan, section, and details.*

second *Werkbund* exposition, the *Weissenhofsiedlung* (a housing development at the Weissenhof), Stuttgart; the other two were for the design of the Glass Industry exhibit, also in Stuttgart; and, with Lilly Reich (1885–1947), a prominent designer, for the *Exposition de la Môde* (Velvet and Silk Cafe), Berlin. In all the commissions, furniture was to play an important role in the definition as well as the articulation of space.

According to its stated purpose, the buildings for the *Weissenhofsiedlung* were intended to exemplify a broad range of housing types. Because Mies did not want the exposition to be either "one-sided or doctrinaire," he invited "the leading representatives of the Modern Movement to make their contributions to the problem of the modern dwelling."[9] The list of participants included Peter Behrens, Victor Bourgeois, Le Corbusier, Richard Döcker, Josef Frank, Walter Gropius, Ludwig Hilberseimer, Pierre Jeanneret (Le Corbusier's brother), J. J. P. Oud, Hans Poelzig, Adolf Rading, Hans Scharoun, Adolf G. Schneck, Mart Stam, Bruno Taut, Max Taut and Mies. They shared a common architectural vocabulary and similar, if not identical, attitudes about form, materials, structure and space. They represented a variety of European nationalities demonstrating to a larger audience that the Modern Movement was not confined to one country, nor was it limited to a few individuals working in isolation.

In terms of housing types, the buildings for the *Weissenhofsiedlung* were not "one-sided." Single-family houses, duplexes, row houses and apartments were constructed. However, in spite of Mies's concern that the exposition not be "doctrinaire," the buildings came to be considered as such. For all the real differences which existed between the work of the various architects, the critics and the general public saw only the similarities—the flat roofs, the predominately white, unadorned surfaces, the simple interiors.

Mies's apartment block, his first steel structure, may have been the clearest expression of the philosophy of the Modern Movement constructed at the exposition: its articulated skeletal structure was clad with light walls which enclosed

43. *Weissenhofsiedlung, Stuttgart, Germany, 1927. Preliminary site model.*

44. *Weissenhofsiedlung. General view.*

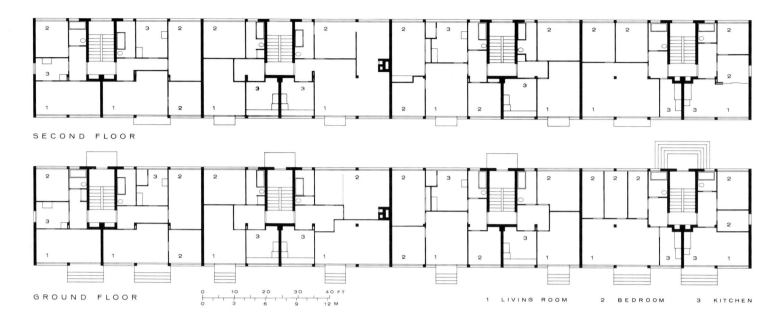

SECOND FLOOR

GROUND FLOOR

0   10   20   30   40 FT
0   3   6   9   12 M

1 LIVING ROOM   2 BEDROOM   3 KITCHEN

47. Apartment building, Weissenhofsiedlung.

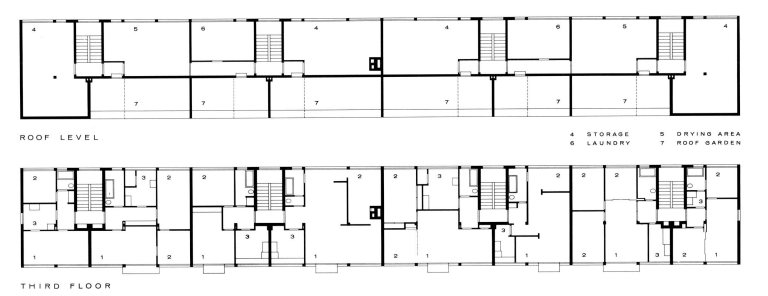

ROOF LEVEL

4 STORAGE 5 DRYING AREA
6 LAUNDRY 7 ROOF GARDEN

THIRD FLOOR

45, 46. Apartment building, Weissenhofsiedlung. Floor plans.

48. Apartment building, Weissenhofsiedlung.

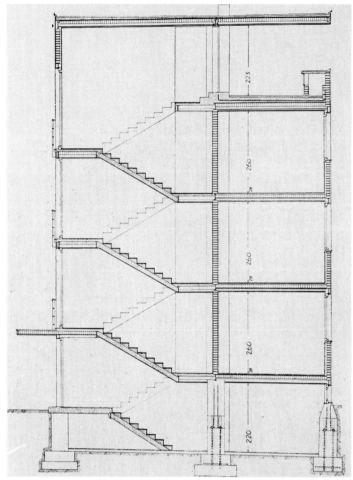

49. *Apartment building, Weissenhofsiedlung. Section through stairway.*

50. *Photomontage of the Weissenhofsiedlung made to resemble an Arab village, ca. 1940. The opponents of the International Style were implying that the style was inferior and suitable only for a non-Aryan people.*

volume rather than defined mass. Materials were selected for their intrinsic worth, their appropriateness to function, and used without applied decoration. Balance was achieved through regularity and proportion rather than from strict reliance on either symmetry or asymmetry.

The open, regular structure of this building, with its moveable interior partitions, allowed for great variety and flexibility in the apartment plans. The grouping of stairways and services—plumbing, electricity and heating—allowed the remaining space to be subdivided according to the needs of the occupants without limiting possible arrangements on floors above or below. As Mies viewed the problem:

"If we regard kitchens and bathrooms, because of their plumbing, as a fixed core, then all other space may be partitioned by means of movable walls."[10]

By contrast the residences designed by Le Corbusier and Pierre Jeanneret, with their exposed columns and living spaces elevated above the ground plane, were clearer in their expression of structure than was Mies in his apartment block. Le Corbusier and Jeanneret appeared reluctant to explore the spatial possibilities suggested by a clear, regular structure, which they had begun to do as early as 1915.

For the *Exposition de la Môde* staged in Berlin, Mies and Frau Lilly Reich[11] defined spaces within the large exhibition hall by draping lengths of black, red, and orange velvet and gold, silver, black, and lemon-yellow silk fabric over straight and curved rods which were suspended from the ceiling. In the café of this exhibition, extensive use of the MR side chairs, with their straight and curved lines, echoed the qualities of the space and reinforced a sense of the whole. With very few elements, they suggested the possibility of a new way of thinking about architectural space as a continuum—an uninterrupted ordered sequence.

The precision, subtlety and assurance reflected in their work implies a working relationship based upon mutual respect, similar sensibilities and complete objectivity. While Mies made dozens of sketches developing a particu-

51. Mies and Le Corbusier engaged in conversation ca. 1927.

52. Apartment building, Weissenhofsiedlung. View of construction.

lar idea or design, Reich sat opposite him offering criticism and making suggestions. Her knowledge of textiles was well known, and she has been credited with suggesting and detailing the continuous caning for the MR side chair and the continuous roll and pleat cushions for the MR lounge chair.[12]

Mies's relationship with Lilly Reich was complex. It included the only professional, working relationship Mies had with a woman, and ultimately it extended to and included their private lives as well. Evidence suggests that she and Mies became lovers late in 1927 or early in 1928.[13] This intimate relationship coupled with their professional one has given rise to speculation regarding the role she may have had in shaping his ideas and/or influencing the direction of his career.

Reich had among Mies's friends and associates both supporters and detractors. Some considered her a sophisticated, energetic, articulate woman, who combined rigorous standards of design with unfailing sensitivity and good taste. Others found her manner and her physical appearance "severe, coarse, peasant-like."[14]

As the daughter of a well-to-do factory owner, she was well traveled and well schooled. In 1902, while attending the *Weiner Werkstätte*, Reich was employed by Josef Hoffmann (1870–1956), its founder and a leading turn-of-the-century Viennese architect. His work was antithetic to the prevailing Art Nouveau style and, with its rectilinear forms and palette of black, white and grays, anticipates the aesthetic concerns and preoccupations of the Modern Movement. Under Hoffmann the *Werkstätte* consisted of a series of

53, 54. *Velvet and Silk Café, Leipzigerstrasse, Berlin, Germany, 1927. Views of the café.*

studios and workshops for the production of utilitarian objects, including furniture. He rejected machine production in favor of handwork, stressed integrity in how materials were used, and believed in the total involvement of the designer from conception through production. With the obvious exception of his attitude toward the machine, Hoffmann's attitude toward the quality of the designed object was very similar to one faction of the *Werkbund's*.

In Reich, Mies found a companion and a professional associate who shared his philosophy about architecture and design. He admired her strength of character, her ability and her accomplishments. These included her appointment to the *Werkbund's* Executive Committee (1921) as its first and only female member and the series of annual exhibitions of exemplary design she directed for the *Werkbund* (1924–27) in Frankfurt.[15]

Before their relationship, Mies had published a few statements which shed some light on his ideas about architecture. These consist of descriptions of three projects (the two Glass Skyscrapers and the Concrete Office Building), some aphorisms on architecture, a statement on industrialization and building, and an essay on the relationship between architecture and the times. Taken as a group, they constitute a complete and mature statement of philosophy of architecture. With few exceptions—the two speeches he delivered in 1930, "The New Era" and "Art Criticism," and his 1940 tribute to Frank Lloyd Wright—Mies's later writings essentially amplified the essence of what he had previously stated: that an incontrovertible relationship exists between architecture and its times, between the method for its realization—technology and materials. Mies described his position to the members of the *Werkbund* meeting in Vienna in 1930:

"The new era is a fact: it exists, irrespective of our 'yes' or 'no.' Yet it is neither better nor worse than any other era. It is pure datum, in itself without value content. Therefore I will not try to define it or clarify its basic structure.

Let us not give undue importance to mechanization and standardization.

54

55. *Mies and Lilly Reich on board an excursion boat on the Wannsee, a lake near Berlin, Germany, 1933.*

Let us accept changed economic and social conditions as a fact.

All these take their blind and fateful course.

One thing will be decisive: the way we assert ourselves in the face of circumstance.

Here the problems of the spirit begin. The important question to ask is not 'what' but 'how.' What goods we produce or what tools we use are not questions of spiritual value.

How the question of skyscrapers versus low buildings is settled, whether we build of steel and glass, are unimportant questions from the point of view of spirit.

Whether we tend to centralization or decentralization in city planning is a practical question, not a question of value.

Yet it is just the question of value that is decisive.

We must set up new values, fix our ultimate goals so that we may establish standards.

For what is right and significant for any era—including the new era—is this: to give the spirit the opportunity for existence."[16]

Reich's influence was, then, less in the realm of ideas than in the application of those ideas to architectural problems which, prior to 1927, Mies was only beginning to address—color, texture and furniture. Not until 1929 did vestiges of her influence appear in his work.

In the two years following the *Weissenhofsiedlung*, Mies's creative activities almost equalled in originality and intensity, his efforts immediately following World War I. Three of the four competitions he entered in 1928 and 1929, the Adam Building on the Leipzigerstrasse, Berlin, and the Office Building on the Friedrichstrasse, Berlin, and the Bank Building, Stuttgart, demonstrate his continuing investigation into the transparent, translucent and reflective qualities of glass. If these projects were more prosaic and practical than the earlier skyscraper projects, it was the result of his growing body of practical experience with glass, especially the Glass Industry's exhibit, Stuttgart (1927).

His other competition entry from this time, the remodeling of the Alexanderplatz, Berlin (1928), was spatially more daring than those of the other competitors. Mies was not content to surround the existing traffic circus with a new facade of buildings. His proposal opened up this important traffic interchange visually and spatially and addressed issues far beyond the scope of the problem. This was comparable to what Schinkel had done earlier in his proposals for the redevelopment of central Berlin. Both Mies and Schinkel understood that new developments in technology will find reflection in the physical structure of the city.

When Mies considered the Alexanderplatz relative to the whole of Berlin's essentially medieval urban structure, the automobile, requirements for light and air, and technology, demanded a new structure, one which could meet

56. *Adam Building, Leipzigerstrasse, Berlin, Germany, 1928. Collage.*

57. *Remodeling of Alexanderplatz, Berlin, Germany, 1928. Collage.*

56

the needs of an industrial society. This he proposed and, in so doing, implied the existence of a larger continuum of which the Alexanderplatz was a part. This was what so impressed Ludwig Hilberseimer (1885–1967), who wrote an important critique of the competition entries, and what no other entrant in the competition either understood or attempted.[17]

All of Mies's work was predicated on technology, its possibilities and its expression. For him technology was the elemental force shaping all aspects of life. Technology provided a system of values both physical and spiritual by which he worked. It was his discipline. It gave clarity, meaning, and structure to his work. As he commented:

". . . it [technology] is a great historical movement. . . . It is, in fact, the essence of our times; the inner-structure of the epoch. There are other things on the side but its essence is the main field of architecture."[18]

The two Krefeld residences, which Mies completed in 1928 for the Esters and Lange families, were simple and commodious. They were each carefully proportioned, bearing wall structures of exposed brick. In each, as in his earlier Wolf house, the size and location of all door and window openings and all interior and exterior dimensions have been determined through his use of a module or ordering device based upon the dimensions of an individual brick and the brick bond itself. His choice of English Bond, with its alternating courses of headers and stretchers (the short and long faces of a brick respectively), comes directly from his experience as a journeyman brick mason, the impact Berlage's Amsterdam Stock Exchange made on him years earlier, and his clients' decision to have brick residences. As Mies described the choice of material:

"I wanted to make this house much more in glass, but the client did not like that. I had great trouble. They were very nice people. We became very good friends. He was president of the silk industry in Germany, but that was to his sorrow. He drank a lot of wine, and so on. That is what you get."[19]

There was in these residences an almost conventional

58. *Remodeling of Alexanderplatz. Collage.*

quality relieved by the understanding of the material they display. But as clear and sensitive as they are, they lack the spatial excitement of his earlier Brick Country House project (1923). The work from these two years pales when compared with his two most important commissions of this period: the German Pavilion for the International Exposition, Barcelona, Spain (1928–29); and the Tugendhat house, Brno, Czechoslovakia (1928–30). While it can be argued that the history of modern architecture may have begun earlier and in other buildings, these two works rank as twentieth-century masterpieces against which all other works of the Modern Movement can be measured.

59. Wolf house, Guben, Germany, 1926.

60. Wolf house.

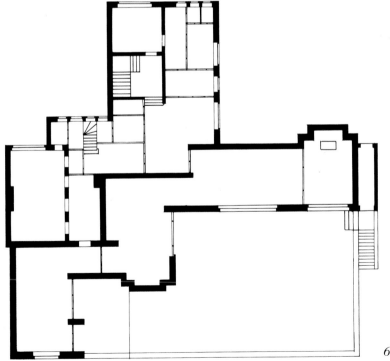

61. Wolf house. Plan.

62. *Country house for Dr. Jürgen Esters, Krefeld, Germany, 1928. Facade.*

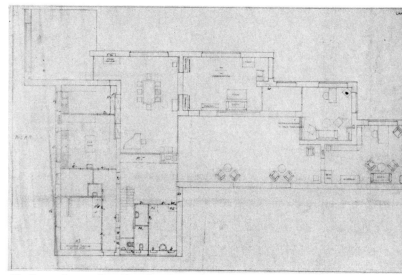

63. *Esters house. Pencil, colored pencil on tracing paper, 19⅞″ x 34⅛″.*

64. *Esters house. View from the garden.*

65. *Hermann Lange house, Krefeld, Germany, 1928. Terrace.*

66. *First Ulrich Lange house, Traar, Germany, 1935. Plan. Pencil on tracing paper, 18½″ x 20⅝″.*

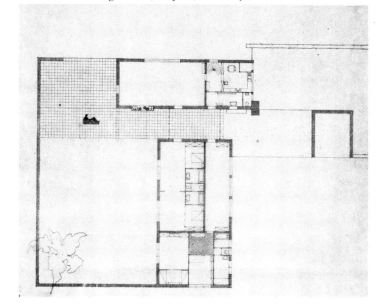

67. *Hermann Lange house. Exterior view with the Esters house in the background.*

68. *Barcelona Pavilion, International Exposition, Barcelona, Spain, 1928–29.*

When Mies and Reich were asked to design the 270 displays for various products and industries for the 10 exhibition spaces allocated to Germany at the exposition in Barcelona, there were no plans for an official reception building.[20] However, the decision by other nations to construct such buildings prompted the German government to commission one in late 1928. Reich, as artistic director of the German section, was already occupied with the design of the industrial exhibits. Mies was therefore free to do the pavilion. As Mies described it:

"Right from the beginning I had had a clear idea of what to do with that pavilion. But nothing was fixed yet, it was still a bit hazy. But then when I visited the showrooms of a marble firm at Hamburg, I said: 'Tell me, haven't you got something else, something really beautiful?' I thought of that freestanding wall I had, and so they said: 'Well, we have a big block of onyx. But that block is sold—to the North German Lloyd.' They want to make big vases from it for the dining room in a new steamer. So I said: 'Listen, let me see it,' and they at once shouted: 'No, no, no, that can't be done, for Heaven's sake you mustn't touch that marvellous piece.' But I said: 'Just give me a hammer, will you, and I'll show you how we used to do that at home.' So reluctantly they brought a hammer, and they were curious whether I would want to chip away a corner. But no, I hit the block hard just once right in the middle, and off came a thin slab the size of my hand. 'Now go and polish it at once so that I*

can see it.' And so we decided to use onyx. We fixed the quantities and bought the stone."[21]

The site he selected allowed for the transverse passage of visitors from a terrace-like avenue bordering the exhibition palaces to the other attractions. In addition, it afforded fine views of the exposition grounds and of the city of Barcelona. The building had no real program, as that term is understood and used by architects today. It was to be whatever Mies chose to make of it. The only function it had to accommodate was a reception for the King and Queen of Spain as they signed the "Golden Book" officially opening the exposition. According to Mies, the furniture designed and fabricated especially for the pavilion, the Barcelona chairs and stools, went unused during the opening ceremony. "To tell you the truth," he remarked, "nobody ever used them."[22]

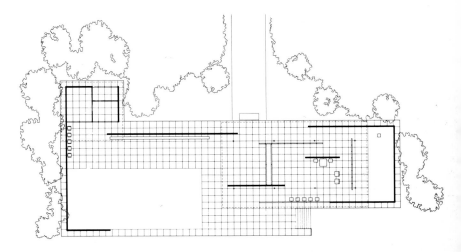

69. Barcelona Pavilion. Plan.

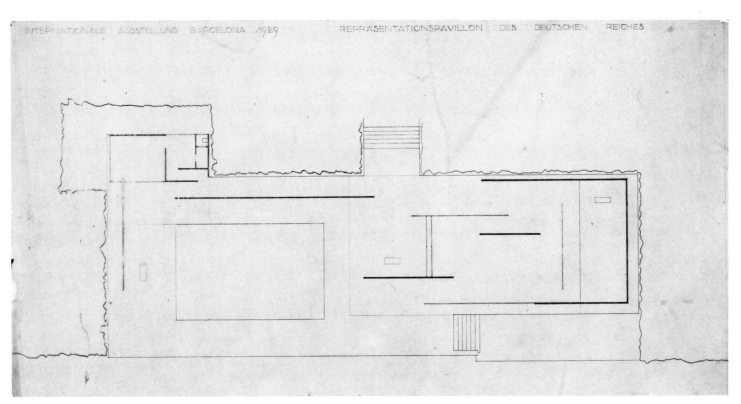

70. Barcelona Pavilion. Plan drawing, first preliminary scheme. Pencil on tracing paper, 19 1/16" x 36".

71. Mies (in top hat) at the ceremonies marking the opening of the International Exposition, Barcelona, 1929.

The first plan for the pavilion (completed very late in 1928) was for a covered area the same size as the one constructed with the roof plane being supported on a series of bearing walls. Spatially, it was not at all unlike the Brick Country House (1923). A second plan utilized both columns and walls to carry the roof load. In the last plan, the one constructed, the weight of the roof plane was carried only on columns; walls became a series of light, non-loadbearing screens. Mies had made the creative leap to the *free plan.* As he described it, "One evening as I was working late on [the Pavilion] I made a sketch of a free-standing wall, and I got a shock. I knew that it was a new principle."[23] The intellectual and visual separation of structural and non-structural building elements allowed for space to be defined and articulated in a new way. Modern architecture has not been the same since. In a real sense, all of his work, beginning as early as 1919 with the first project for the Glass Skyscraper, led him to the discovery of this "principle," the free plan, as he called it.

Independent of Mies, Le Corbusier had made a similar discovery which he clarified and articulated in 1926 in his *"Les 5 Points d'une architecture nouvelle"* (the 5 points of the new architecture). It was as if the idea was in the air looking for a fertile mind (or minds) in which to take root and grow. But no other architect—not even Le Corbusier in the Villa Savoye (1929–30)—so carefully and so completely explored the subtle structural and spatial relationships made possible once walls were freed from their load-bearing function and allowed to become light screens or planes in space.

In its precision and refinement, the pavilion was an apotheosis of German craftsmanship and industry, a metaphor for technology in the twentieth century. The possibility that a piece of architecture might embody and reflect technology as the driving force of society was either ignored or overlooked by the critics. It was not a new idea for Mies: as early as 1924, he had postulated the relationship between architecture and its place in time. He wrote:

"Greek temples, Roman basilicas and medieval cathedrals

64

72. *The departure of the King and Queen of Spain from the opening of the International Exposition in Barcelona. Mies's pavilion was the site of the opening ceremonies.*

73. *International Exposition, Barcelona. The Silk exhibit for the German section, designed by Lilly Reich with Mies.*

are significant to us as creations of a whole epoch rather than as works of individual architects. Who asks the names of these builders? Of what significance are the fortuitous personalities of their creators? Such buildings are impersonal by their very nature. They are pure expressions of their time. Their true meaning is that they are symbols of their epoch." [24]

In Barcelona, Mies was able to represent this *idea* three-dimensionally in the clearest possible way because the abstract nature of the building's program allowed him to concentrate totally on the *idea* of space.

As the three-dimensional realization of an idea (or space), the pavilion existed for only a few months. Shortly after the exposition ended, it was dismantled. Salvageable parts were sold in Barcelona or shipped to Germany for reuse there. [25] Because few critics or historians actually visited the pavilion during its eight-month existence, much of what was later written about it was done from photographs. As Juan Bonta pointed out (1975), it was not until long after the fact that the pavilion's importance was recognized. Then, almost overnight, it went from critical limbo to become one of the most important [significant] buildings of the Modern Movement [twentieth century]. [26] Historians

realized that with the Barcelona Pavilion, as this building for the German government is more generally known, Mies demonstrated a new idea about space predicated on the technology of modern industrialism and the spirit of the times. [27]

The few contemporary descriptions of the pavilion focus more attention on Mies's use of marble, onyx and travertine than on the space he created. For many critics his use of traditional building materials appeared to be a rejection of the aesthetic with which the Modern Movement was identified. But such an attitude reduces modern architecture to white walls with unadorned surfaces using reinforced concrete or steel—especially chrome-plated steel—for its structure. Modern architecture was and remains much more than that.

Other critics found in Mies's skillful handling of traditional and new materials an attempt by a "modern" architect to develop an architecture which appealed to the senses, especially the eyes, as well as the intellect. [28] But few went beyond this to understand that the conceptual originality of the space and the tension created by the placement of load-bearing and nonload-bearing elements were more important than the materials Mies used to create space.

66

One American critic did understand what Germany and Mies accomplished in Barcelona. In her contemporary account of the exposition, Helen Appleton Read wrote:

"Of nations represented, Germany alone symbolized her industrial and cultural status in a modern gesture.

Germany naturally made a special effort in her first entry into an international affair since the War. Her contribution is more than putting her best foot forward. Her austerely elegant pavilion designed by Mies Van Der Rohe, pioneer in the Modern Movement in architecture, is a symbol of Germany's post-war Kultur, *a convincing exposition of the aesthetique of modern architecture. The technical and industrial dis-*

74. *International Exposition, Barcelona. The Silk exhibit.*

plays, also arranged by Mies, have that clarity and objectivity characteristic of Germany's present point of view. They symbolize the German Kommissar, Dr. Von Schnitzler's explanation of the intention of Germany's representation.

'We have wanted to show here what we can do, what we are and how we feel and see today. We do not want anything more than Clarity, Simplicity and Integrity.'

To plan a building which shall represent purely the idea of Sachlichkeit [objectivity] and shall serve no utilitarian purpose, is an unusual, difficult assignment because it necessitates working without a disciplinary control entailed by a specific practical problem. That German officialdom had the good judgment to choose Mies is significant of her post-war culture.

Radical rationalist that he is, his designs are governed by a passion for beautiful architecture. He is one of the very few modern architects who has carried its theories beyond a barren functional formula into the plastically beautiful. Material and space disposition are the ingredients with which he gets his effect of elegant serenity. Evincing in his work a love for beautiful materials and textures he emphasizes this predilection."[29]

Read understood what others did not: that Mies's use of materials was based on their appropriateness to function and on aesthetics rather than their properties in a polemic. Thus freed from short-lived social or political considerations, his work addressed questions of a more general and timeless nature.

Because the pavilion was conceived as a continuum, it transcended the physical limitations of its site as well as the physical definition of space which walls, floors and roof planes traditionally made. There was no inside to this building. There was only the phenomenon of a more defined outside. The space Mies created had the characteristic of a Möbius strip in that, as one moved through it, what was first perceived as inside was, in actuality, outside. Mies was clearly aware of this ambiguity, Mies had two pairs of doors, traditional architectural elements used

to help define inside from outside, removed for the official photographs. Only the surface mounted hinges in the floor and ceiling betrayed the doors' existence.

Those spatial and architectural qualities in the Barcelona Pavilion which might be accepted by some or admired by others were, at once, controversial in the Tugendhat house. The aesthetics of a "functionless" space could not, according to some of Mies's critics, be applied to the problems of the "modern" house. These same critics, apparently, had not noticed what Mies was advocating, functionally and spatially, in the *Weissenhofsiedlung* apartment block (1927). They missed the subtle spatial direction his work had taken once walls were liberated from their bearing function and became planes, with a building's weight now carried on light steel columns.

Mies described the commission and how it came to be given to him in 1959 at a general meeting of the Architectural Association in London:

"Mr. Tugendhat came to me. First, he received this house as a wedding present. He was a very careful man and he was sick. He did not believe in one doctor only: he had three. He had looked at houses, and he wanted to find an architect. He picked me out for a curious reason. He saw a house which I built when I was very young, when I was about twenty years old. It was very well built, and so on. He liked that. He expected something similar. He came to me and talked with me. I went there and saw the situation. I designed the house. I remember that it was on Christmas Eve when he saw the design of the house. He nearly died! But his wife was interested in art; she had some of Van Gogh's pictures. She said, 'Let us think it over.' Tugendhat could have thrown her out.

However, on New Year's Eve he came to me and told me that he had thought it over and I should go ahead with the house. We had some trouble about it at the time, but we can take that for granted. He said that he did not like this open space; it would be too disturbing; people would be there when he was in the library with his great thoughts. He was a business man, I think. I said: 'Oh, all right. We will try it

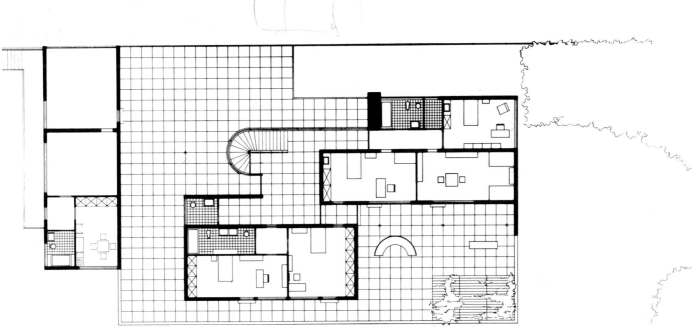

75, 76. *Tugendhat house, Brno, Czechoslovakia, 1928–30.*
Entrance and lower level plans.

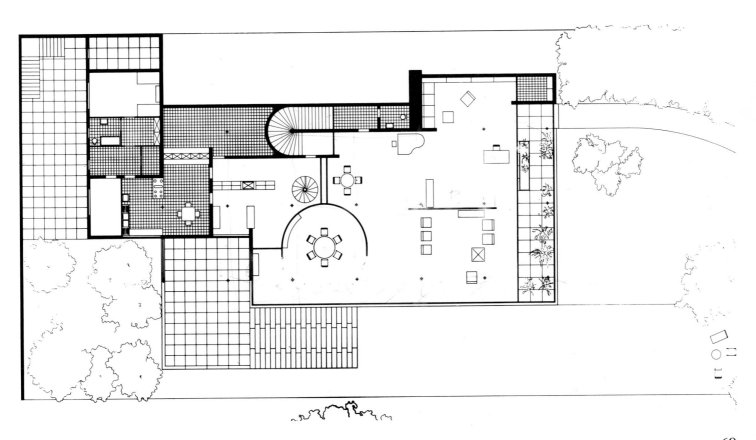

77. *Tugendhat house. Perspective sketch.*

78. *Tugendhat house. View from the garden.*

out and, if you do not want it, we can close the rooms in. We can put in glass walls. It will be the same.' We tried it. We put wooden scaffold pieces up. He was listening in his library and we were talking just normally. He did not hear anything.

Later he said to me: 'Now I give in on everything, but not about the furniture.' I said, 'This is too bad.' I decided to send furniture to Brno from Berlin. I said to my superintendent: 'You keep the furniture and shortly before lunch call him out and say that you are at his house with furniture. He will be furious, but you must expect that.' He said, 'Take it out,' before he saw it. However, after lunch he liked it. I think we should treat our clients as children, not as architects.[30]

For a family of the Tugendhats' affluence and position, the building program was complex and extensive. There were the requisite servants' quarters; children's wing with provisions for a governess; master suite with separate, interconnected bedrooms; kitchen, servants' hall and butler's pantry; living room, dining room, library, study and music room; darkroom; entry hall and stairway; and a garage and quarters for a chauffeur.

Taking advantage of the sloped site, Mies separated the private sleeping areas from domestic and social areas. The resulting two-story residence allowed for the possibility of developing different, but related, spatial ideas on each floor. The upper or bedroom and entry level presents a solid, relatively windowless one-story facade to the street. What appear as two elements on a terrace connected by an

70

79. Tugendhat house. Exterior.

open, roofed area are, in actuality, three pavilion-like structures arranged on a plane in such a way as to define other exterior spaces—public as in the entry, or private as in the vine-covered play area for the children.

Mies used the stairway's curved wall of etched glass to connect the two solid bedroom elements to each other and to create a foyer. This same curved wall of translucent etched glass simultaneously defines and conceals the entry in a manner reminiscent of Frank Lloyd Wright's early work. But Mies's placement of elements on the upper level of the house defines exterior spaces in a manner anticipating his master plan for the Illinois Institute of Technology (1940–41) by ten years.

The lower level of the house was spatially richer and architecturally more ambitious. Its regular structure of exposed chromium-sheathed steel columns was articulated by curved and straight planes of ebony, onyx and glass. With these simple elements, Mies added a new dimension to the possibilities of the free plan. The nonload-bearing wall-planes and columns define spaces within a larger whole accommodating a variety of functions. The addition of more and various types of furniture (dining and game tables, a desk, benches, storage cabinets of Mies's design and a piano) has, on this floor of the house, clarified the spatial ambiguity of the Barcelona Pavilion without diminishing Mies's idea that a building with its wall, roof and floor planes only *defines* a portion of a larger spatial continuum without *limiting* it.

With the Tugendhat house, traditional definitions of "room" and "function" lost their meaning: "space" and "functional" took on new meaning. As critics attempted to describe or evaluate Mies's work, the limitations of traditional criteria and definitions became clear. As they asked, "Can one live in the Tugendhat House?" even the idea of living changed and took on a new meaning. In Ludwig Hilberseimer's opinion, the answer as to how one "lives" in the house ultimately rested with the Tugendhats.[31] Walter Riezler concurred. For him, this building represented both a new approach to building and a new definition for "room"

72

80. Tugendhat house. Wall section showing electrically retractable plate glass window.

82, 83. Tugendhat house. Views of the entrance.

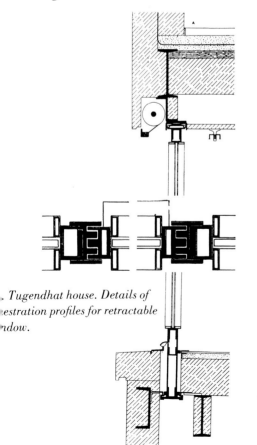

. Tugendhat house. Details of
estration profiles for retractable
ndow.

74

84. *Tugendhat house. View of the living and dining space showing portions of the exterior glass wall lowered out of sight.*

85. *Tugendhat house. Library.*

[function].[32] However, Justus Bier's stance was more traditional: he concluded his objections to the openness of the major living area by comparing this space to an "exhibition space."[33]

It was, however, Hilberseimer who saw further and understood with greater insight. For him the importance of this residence was not that it was a specific solution to a specific set of programmatic requirements. Its importance lay in the "manner [architectural means] in which the specific solution had been achieved [realized]." It was its general, rather than its specific nature, which appealed to him.[34]

In addition to demonstrating Mies's mastery of the free

plan, both the Tugendhat house and the Barcelona Pavilion are important because in them we can at last see Reich's influence. Previously, Mies was cautious in his use of color and texture. But as Reich commented, "One must have courage for color."[35] She gave Mies that courage. Contemporary black and white photographs do not begin to convey the visual and textural richness of these two buildings.

In the Barcelona Pavilion, Mies combined green Tinian and vert antique marbles; Roman travertine; a tawny onyx; clear, gray, and bottle-green glass; a black (wool?) rug; a red (silk?) drape with furniture—the famous Barcelona Chair—upholstered in white kid leather. In the Tugendhat

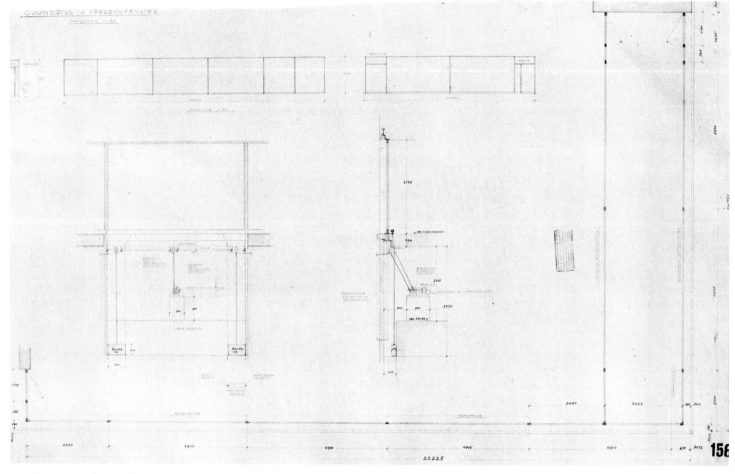

86. Tugendhat house. Window wall details. Pencil on print, 31⅜" x 50⅝".

house, the floor of the major living space was covered with white linoleum. The glass walls were draped with a silver-gray Shantung silk; and the space was divided by a linear plane of tawny-gold onyx and a curved plane of black and pale brown Macassar ebony. The various pieces of furniture, including two chairs specifically designed for the house—the Tugendhat Chair and the Brno Chair—were upholstered in a silver-gray fabric, emerald green cowhide, ruby-red velvet, or white calf parchment. A natural wool rug and oriental rugs covered portions of the linoleum-

covered floor.[36] These are nothing if not courageous combinations of color and texture.

It is worth noting that despite their machine-made appearance, the Barcelona and Tugendhat Chairs were essentially handmade in limited quantities. Their cantilevered structures of compound curves of chromium plated steel bars were too complex to be fabricated except by hand. The connections, especially in the Barcelona Chair, demanded precision and accuracy. As a result, the connections were welded, ground and polished by hand. Despite the fact that

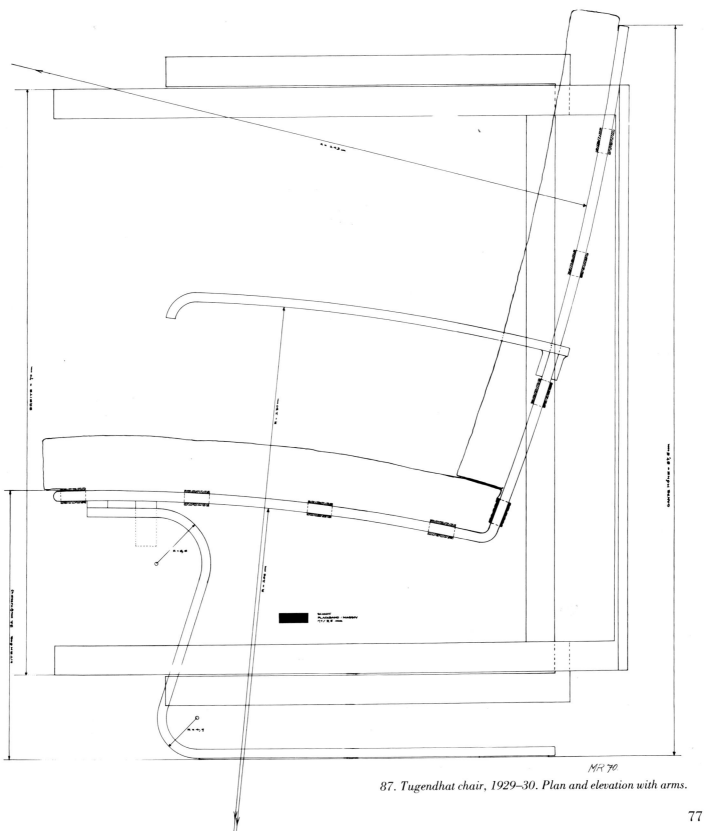

87. *Tugendhat chair, 1929–30. Plan and elevation with arms.*

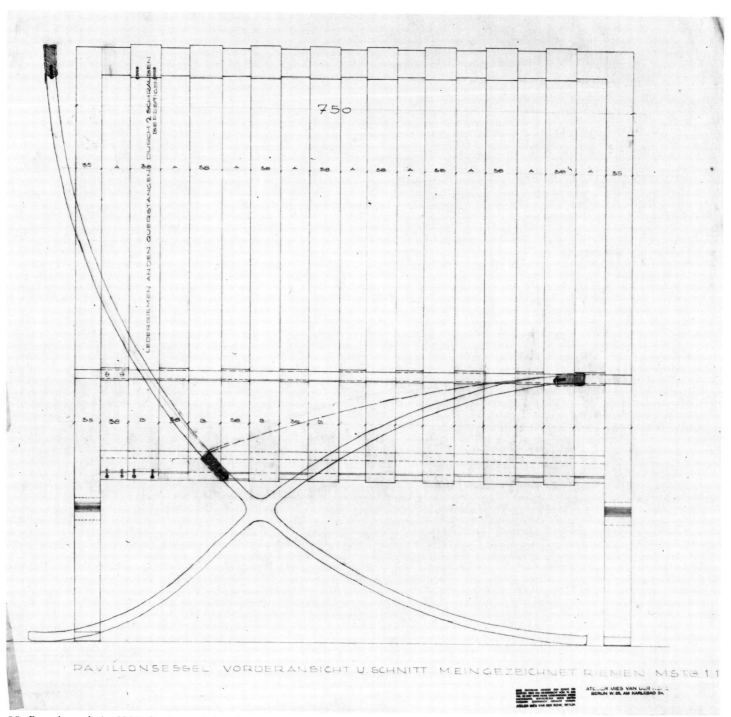

88. Barcelona chair, 1929. Section and elevation.

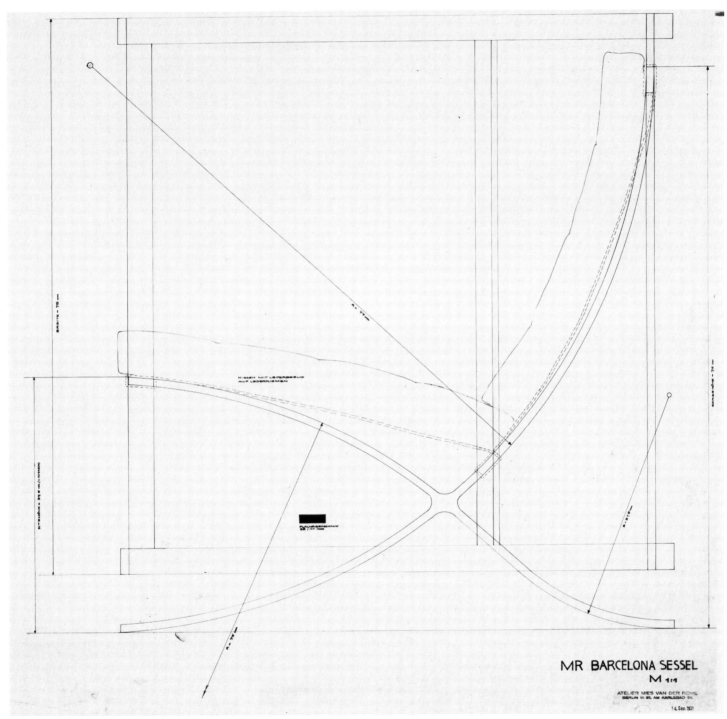

MR BARCELONA SESSEL
M 1:1

ATELIER MIES VAN DER ROHE
BERLIN W. 35, AM KARLSBAD 24

14. Sep. 1931

89. Barcelona chair, 1929. Plan and elevation.

79

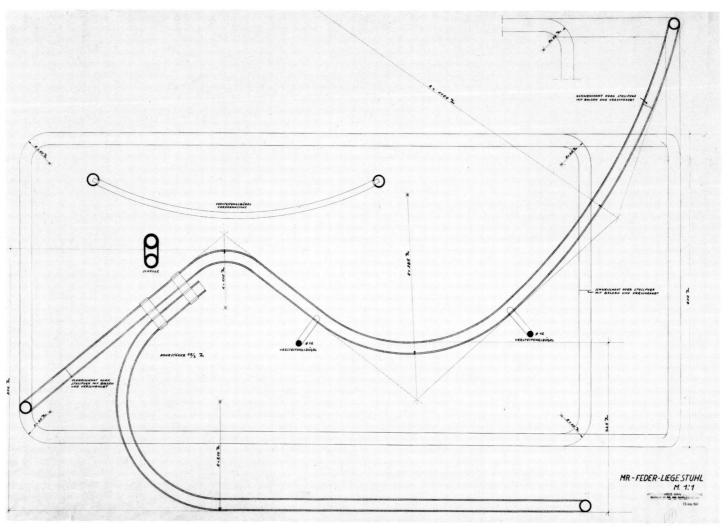

90. *MR chaise longue with spring frame, 1931.*
Plan, section, and details.

it is handcrafted, the Barcelona Chair, among all Mies's furniture, became the symbol for a technological age. Prized for its enduring beauty, it remains the hallmark of luxury, elegance and craftsmanship.

Immediately following the close of the exposition in Barcelona, Mies was asked to design a small, freestanding residence for one person as part of the *Werkbund's* 1931 Berlin Building Exposition and for which he and Reich designed a number of other exhibits. Mies's House for a

Bachelor was a logical extension and a continuation of the spatial idea embraced in both the Barcelona Pavilion and the Tugendhat house. Mies developed this plan almost as if to answer those critics of the free plan who questioned whether various domestic functions with their requirements for visual and/or auditory privacy could be contained within the limits of a more modest building program and limited space.

A series of regular structural bays has been exposed be-

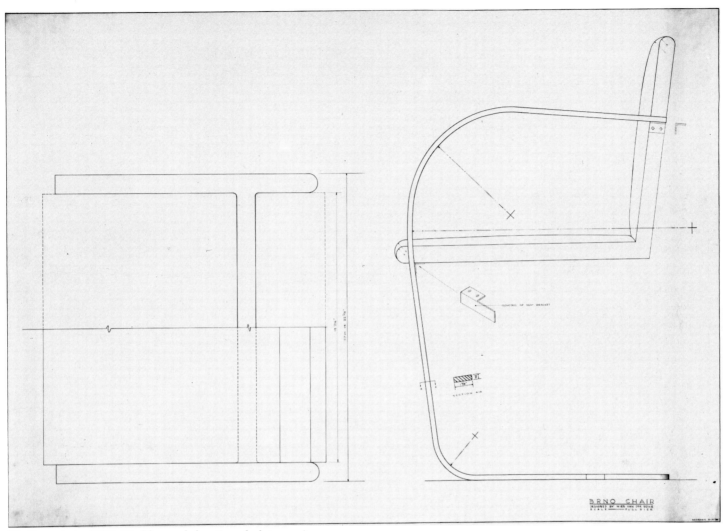

BRNO CHAIR
DESIGNED BY MIES VAN DER ROHE
SCALE ———— FULL SIZE

91. *Brno chair, 1929–30. Plan and elevation of a later version*
designed in steel bar stock rather than tubular steel.

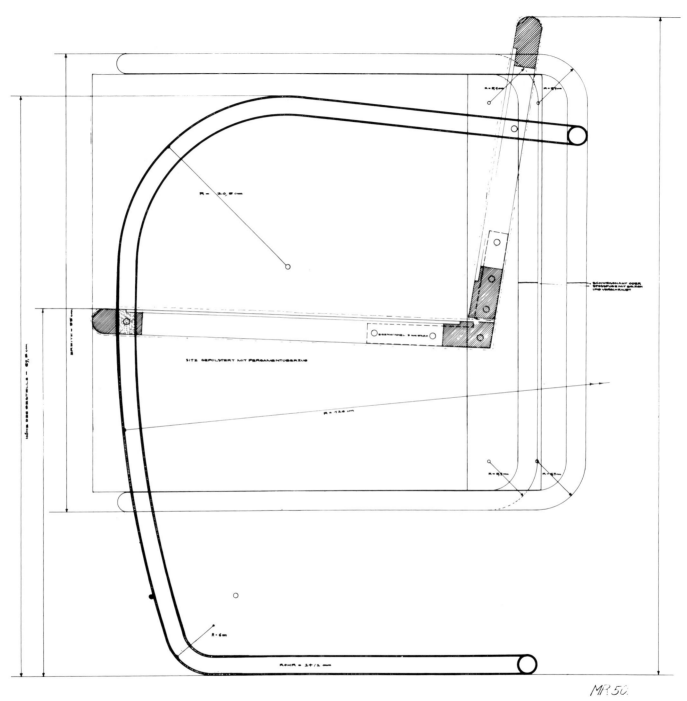

92. Brno chair. Plan and section of the tubular steel version.

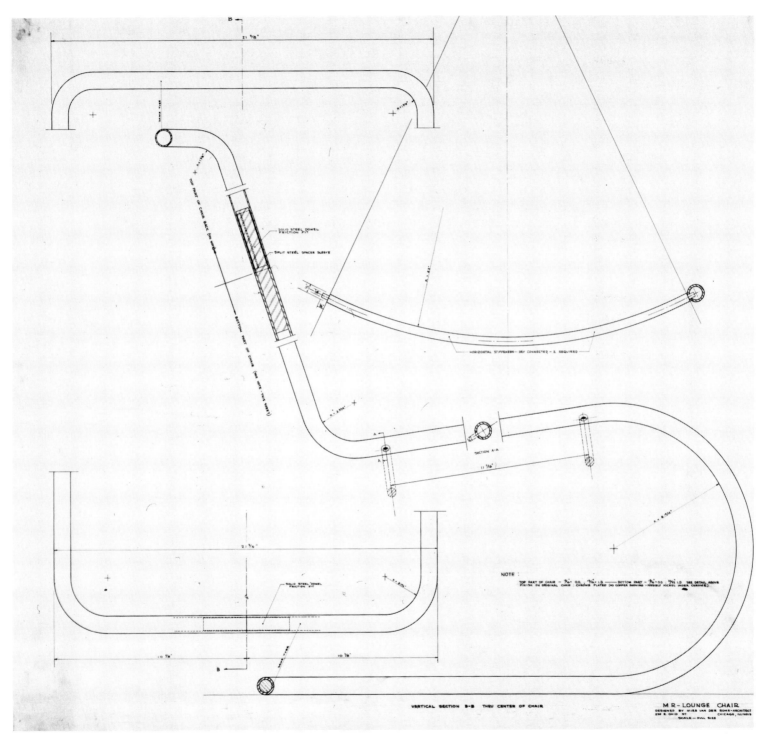

93. *MR lounge chair, 1931. Plan, section, and details.*

neath a rectangular roof plane. Nonload-bearing walls pass beneath the roof and define spaces within the perimeter of the roof and beyond. With the obvious exception of the service functions—baths, kitchens and servant's bedroom—none of the spaces has been completely enclosed with solid walls. This house, like its predecessor the Brick Country House (1923), included the space which extended beyond the area defined by the roof to incorporate the landscape itself.

With the 1931 Berlin Building Exposition, the Modern Movement demonstrated a mature statement of design intentions and a clear record of achievement. The critics'

94. House for a Bachelor, Berlin Building Exposition, Berlin, Germany, 1931. Exterior view.

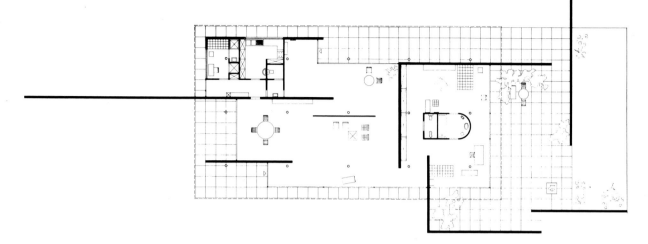

95, 96. House for a Bachelor. Plan and interior.

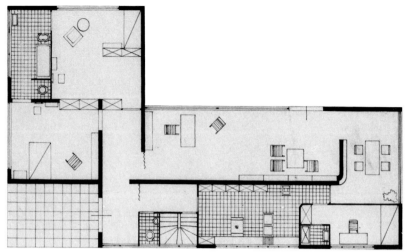

97. *Plan of model house for a couple without children.*
Berlin Building Exposition. Lilly Reich, 1931.

reaction in Berlin to the light, simple, open interior characteristic of the Modern Movement was not quite the *horror vacui* it had once been. There appeared to be understanding and appreciation of the aesthetics and possibilities modern architecture offered. It came at an important turning point in the history of modern architecture in Europe.

While Henry-Russell Hitchcock's and Philip Johnson's (1932) exhibition, "The International Style" at the Museum of Modern Art in New York (and their subsequent monograph of the same title),[37] did much to promote the cause of modern architecture in the United States, forces were already at work in Germany which would result in the total rejection of the structure, content, and the aesthetics of the Modern Movement. The chauvinism dormant in Germany since the end of World War I was reawakened and nurtured by the lingering and debilitating affects of the terms of the Treaty of Versailles and the impotency of the Weimar government in the face of the Great Depression. As social, political and economic conditions worsened, there came a call for a return to the restoration of a national identity, for *völkisch* (national or pure German) architecture and *Blut und Boden*[38] (blood and soil) interiors. The "international" scope of modern architecture was rejected in favor of an architecture which would serve nationalistic ends.

As Germany was beginning to reject the Modern Movement, Mies's European career reached its zenith. In 1930 at the recommendation of Walter Gropius, founder of the Bauhaus, Mies was appointed director of that institution. The following year he was elected to the Prussian Academy of Arts and Sciences. As a leader of the Modern Movement, his selection to head the Bauhaus was logical and in the best interest of a school wracked by political anarchy and near collapse.

The Bauhaus had been founded in 1919 at the behest of the duke of Sachen-Weimar-Eisenach. Gropius merged two existing arts and crafts schools into a new school called *Das Staatliche Bauhaus Weimar.* The philosophy of design education at the Bauhaus was predicated on two important and interrelated concepts: that artists are craftsmen to whom the responsibility for fulfilling specific aesthetic and functional needs has been given; that the machine, primary tool for production, when combined with techniques for mass-production, is to be used in the development of those products, e.g., utilitarian goods, furniture, wall coverings, fabrics, jewelry, etc., appropriate to an industrial society.

The Bauhaus embodied as well as realized the aims of the *Werkbund.* It became, through its experiments and innovations in design education and the quality of its faculty, one of the most important, if not the most important, influences on design in the twentieth century. No aspect of life or design from teacups to city planning went unstudied there.

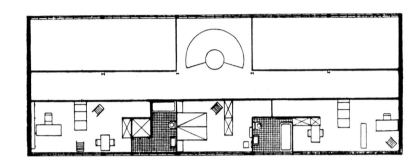

98. *Apartment at the Berlin Building Exposition furnished by Lilly Reich.*

And what the Bauhaus proposed in terms of design challenged the status quo and how life might be lived.

With the encouragement and support of the mayor of Dessau, Fritz Hesse, Gropius moved the school there from Wiemar in 1925. Dessau provided a cultural climate which was more receptive to what the Bauhaus represented. But the challenges the Bauhaus presented to education and society did not disappear with a change of location. The curriculum underwent changes in an attempt to silence its critics; additional faculty members were appointed including Hannes Meyer (1889–1954) in 1927 to head the newly formed department of architecture. An uneasy stability was achieved, and in 1928 Gropius decided to resign. At his recommendation and with the concurrence of the Dessau City Council, Meyer was appointed as his successor. With Gropius's departure, though, three important faculty members left the school: Herbert Bayer (1900–   ), László Moholy-Nagy (1895–1946) and Marcel Breuer. As a result, when Meyer took over as director of the school, not only was he confronted with the usual problems of transition and adjustment, but he also had to fill these three vacancies.

As Hans Wingler described the situation:

"The new group that had gathered around the Director [Meyer] lacked the homogeneity necessary to sustain the Bauhaus. The fact that the Director forfeited his authority brought the danger of stagnation to the coöperative effort and of chaotic dissolution of the entire institute." [39]

But Wingler may have exaggerated the situation. It is true that the school was in a state of flux; it is also true that the municipal authorities had requested certain changes in the curriculum's structure and content. For two years Meyer worked to achieve order and stability. However, lacking the political and organizational skills necessary to achieve stability and at the request of the authorities, Meyer resigned in 1930. The city council tried to persuade Gropius to again head up the school; instead he suggested Mies who was appointed director in 1930.

As soon as Mies was appointed, he took "stringent steps to restore order which the political activities and lack of discipline of part of the student body at the Bauhaus had disturbed."[40] With Mayor Hesse's support, the school was closed for several weeks, during which time Mies interviewed every student, dismissing those who were not serious or who were merely political agitators. At first there was resistance to Mies's forceful approach which was in sharp contrast to Meyer's. A small group of students demanded that Mies exhibit his work so that they could judge whether or not he was fit to head the school. Mies did not comply with this demand. Instead, he convinced the skeptics among the students and faculty of the wisdom of his appointment through reason and the strength of his personality and integrity. Soon the faculty and students began to understand Mies and accept his direction. Ultimately, they held him in high regard.

Under Mies the manufacture of various items bearing the Bauhaus imprimatur was halted almost completely. Mies was then able to concentrate the resultant savings both in money and man power on teaching. For him the most important task confronting the Bauhaus was the consolidation and rationalization of the school's existing methods and means.[41] Many of the workshops were restructured and the number of faculty reduced. With the exception of

Reich, no new appointments were made until the end of the Dessau Bauhaus. Just as there was resistance to the *Werkbund*, so there was resistance to the *idea* which directed the Bauhaus.

As early as 1931, the National Socialists began a carefully orchestrated campaign of harassment against the Bauhaus. After local elections, they gained control of the Dessau City Council and moved to close the school. In 1953 while talking with some students, Mies recalled the events surrounding the closing of the Bauhaus:

"It was like this. Anhalt was the first state in Germany with a

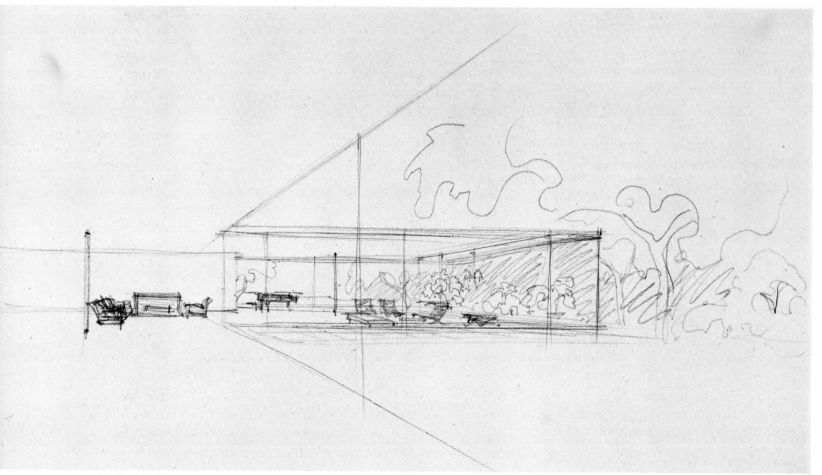

99. Gericke house, Wannsee, Berlin, Germany, 1930. Perspective sketch of the living room.

88

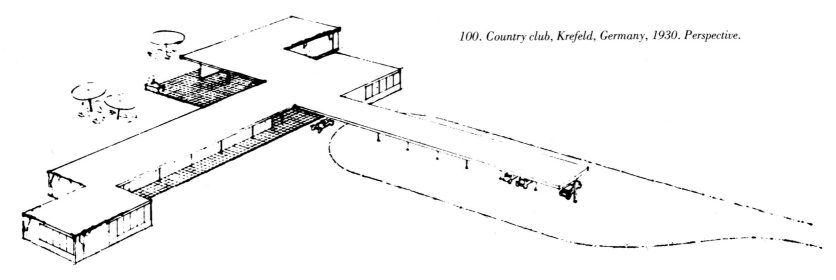

100. Country club, Krefeld, Germany, 1930. Perspective.

National-Socialist government, and the Bauhaus was under state control, though it was supported by the democratic council of Dessau—and that also went National-Socialist. They said they'd come with a Commission to inspect the school, and the mayor asked if I'd rather go on holiday at that time etc. I said: 'No, I'd rather like to see these people.' So we put on a first-class exhibition, probably the best the Bauhaus ever did. But the decision, of course, had been made long before. It was now only a formality if the Commission came to look at our things. They no doubt then made a devastating report, and that was the end of it."[42]

Given the political instability of 1932, the Nazis could easily have arranged the dissolution of the Bauhaus by the end of the year. However, such was the extent of their hatred for the Bauhaus that they were unwilling to wait even a few months to achieve their ends. Their impatience worked in Mies's favor. He was able to force compliance with the existing contractual obligations between the city of Dessau and the school: faculty salaries were to continue to be paid, and limited quantities of tools and means of instruction were to be provided. Mies was also able to assume personal responsibility for the Bauhaus and to move it to Berlin as a private school.

It is an indication of Mies's political naiveté that he thought Berlin would provide the climate and anonymity necessary for the school's continued existence. Late in 1932 classes were resumed, and Mies reopened the school.

"*. . . I rented a factory in Berlin. I did that on my own. It cost me 27,000 marks for three years. It cost 9,000 marks a year. That was a lot of money in Germany, nothing in America. So I rented this factory that was terrible, black. We started to work—all of us—every student. Many Americans who were with us will remember that we cleaned it all up and painted everything white. This was a solid, simple factory painted clean, wonderful, you know. And just on the outside, on the street, there was a broken down wooden fence, closed. You couldn't see the building. And I can assure you there were a lot of people when they came there and they saw this fence went home. But the good ones, they came through and stayed. They didn't care about the fence. We had a wonderful group of students.*"[43]

For ten months there was relative calm. Then:

"*One morning, I had to come from Berlin in the streetcar and walk a little, and I had to pass over the bridge from which you would see our building, I nearly died. It was so wrong. Our wonderful building was surrounded by Gestapo—black uniforms—with bayonets. It was really surrounded. I ran to be there. And a sentry said, 'Stop here.' I said, 'What? This is my factory. I rented it. I have a right to see it.'*

'You are the owner? Come in.' He knew I never would come out if they didn't want me to. Then I went and talked to the

officer. I said, 'I am the director of this school,' and he said, 'Oh, come in,' and we talked some more and he said, 'You know there was an affair against the mayor of Dessau and we are just investigating the documents of the founding of the Bauhaus.' I said, 'Come in.' I called all the people and said, 'Open everything for inspection, open everything.' I was certain there was nothing there that could be misinterpreted.

The investigation took hours. In the end the Gestapo became so tired and hungry that they called their headquarters and said, 'What should we do? Should we work here forever? We are hungry and so on.' And they were told, 'Lock it and forget it.'

Then I called up Alfred Rosenberg. He was the party philosopher of the Nazis' culture, and he was the head of the movement. It was called Bund Deutsche Kultur. I called him up and said, 'I want to talk with you.' He said, 'I am very busy.'

'I understand that, but even so, at any time you tell me I will be there.'

'Could you be here at eleven o'clock tonight?'

'Certainly.'

My friends, Hilberseimer and Lilly Reich and some other people said, 'You will not be so stupid as to go there at eleven o'clock?' They were afraid, you know, that they would just kill me or do something. 'I am not afraid. I have nothing. I'd like to talk with this man.'

So I went that night and we really talked, you know, for an hour. And my friends, Hilberseimer and Lilly Reich were sitting across the street in a café window so they could see when I came out, if alone, or under guards, or what.

I told Rosenberg the Gestapo had closed the Bauhaus and I wanted to have it open again. I said, 'You know, the Bauhaus has a certain idea and I think that it is important. It has nothing to do with politics or anything. It has something to do with technology.' And then for the first time he told me about himself. He said, 'I am a trained architect from the Baltic states, from Riga.' He had a diploma as an

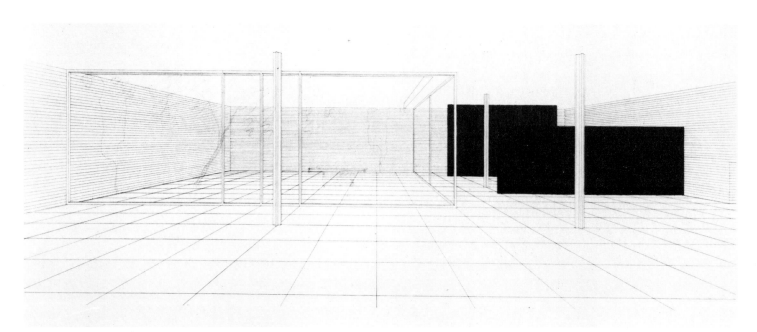

101. Row house, 1931. Perspective from the living room.

architect from Riga. I said, 'Then we certainly will understand each other.' And he said, 'Never! What do you expect me to do? You know the Bauhaus is supported by forces that are fighting our forces. It is one army against another, only in the spiritual field.' And I said, 'No, I really don't think it is like that.' And he said, 'Why didn't you change the name, for heaven's sake, when you moved the Bauhaus from Dessau to Berlin?' I said, 'Don't you think the Bauhaus is a wonderful name? You cannot find a better one.' He said, 'I don't like what the Bauhaus is doing. I know you can suspend, you can cantilever something, but my feeling demands a support." I said, 'Even if it is cantilevered?' And he said, 'Yes.' He wanted to know, 'What is it you want to do at the Bauhaus?' I said, 'Listen, you are sitting here in an important position. And look at your writing table, this shabby writing table. Do you like it? I would throw it out of the window. That is what we want to do. We want to have good objects that we have not to throw out of the window.' And he said, 'I will see what I can do for you.' I said, 'Don't wait too long.'

Then from there on I went every second day for three months to the headquarters of the Gestapo. I had the feeling that I had the right. That was my school. It was a private school. I signed the contract. It was 27,000 marks—a lot of money. And when they closed it I said, 'I will not give up that thing.' And it took me three months, exactly three months, to get to the head of the Gestapo. He must have had a back door somewhere, you know. And he had a bench in the waiting room not wider than four inches, to make you tired so that you would go home again. But one day I got him. He was young, very young . . . and he said, 'Come in. What do you want?' I said, 'I would like to talk to you about the Bauhaus. What is going on? You have closed the Bauhaus. It is my private property, and I want to know for what reason. We didn't steal anything. We didn't make a revolution. I'd like to know how can that be.'

'Oh,' he said, 'I know you perfectly, and I am very interested in the movement, the Bauhaus movement, and so on, but we don't know what is with Kandinsky.'[44] I said, 'I make all the

102. Mies teaching at the Dessau Bauhaus prior to October 1, 1932, when the school closed.

103. *Ludwig Hilberseimer (left) and Mies celebrating in the garden of a Wannsee restaurant, 1933.*

guarantee about Kandinsky.' He said, 'You have to, but be careful. We don't know anything about him, but if you want to have him it is O.K. with us. But if something happens, we pick up you.' He was very clear about that. I said, 'That is all right. Do that.' And then he said, 'I will talk with Goering, because I am really interested in this school.' And I really believe he was."[45]

Reopening the school was not quite so simple. Among the conditions demanded by the leadership of the Third Reich were the dismissal of Hilberseimer, Mies's friend and colleague, and Kandinsky, the appointment of Nazi sympathizers, revision of the syllabus, and completion of questionnaires by all staff.[46]

It was not clear even to Mies that the Bauhaus would be closed sooner or later. Having described the faculty as "cultural Bolsheviks," Hitler could hardly be sympathetic to the rational and objective approach to design which was the hallmark of the Bauhaus. As he wrote in *Mein Kampf* (1925–27):

"Since the masses have only a poor acquaintance with abstract ideas, their reactions lie more in the domain of feelings, where the roots of their positive as well as their negative attitudes furnish the reason for their extraordinary stability. It is always more difficult to fight against faith than knowledge. And the driving force which has brought about the most tremendous revolution on this earth has never been a body of scientific teaching which has gained power over the masses, but always a devotion which has inspired them, and often a kind of hysteria which has urged them to action. Whoever wishes to win over the masses must know the key that will open the door to their hearts. It is not objectivity, which is a feckless attitude, but a determined will, backed up by power where necessary."[47]

To all intents and purposes, when Hitler assumed leadership of the government, he assumed absolute control over all facets of German life including art, architecture and design.

As a matter of principle, Mies wanted the faculty, not the

government, to determine the fate of the school.

"Finally I got a letter saying we could open the Bauhaus again. When I got this letter I called Lilly Reich. I said, 'I got a letter. We can open the school again. Order champagne.' She said, 'What for? We don't have money.' I said, 'Order champagne.' I called the faculty together: Albers, Kandinsky . . . they were still around us, you know, and some other people: Hilberseimer, Peterhans, and I said, 'Here is the letter from the Gestapo that we open the Bauhaus again.' They said, 'That is wonderful.' I said, 'Now, I went there for three months every second day just to get this letter. I was anxious to get this letter. I wanted to have the permission to go ahead. And now I make a proposition, and I hope you will agree with me. I will write them a letter back: 'Thank you very much for the permission to open the school again, but the faculty has decided to close it!'

I had worked on it for this moment. It was the reason I

ordered champagne. Everybody accepted it, and was delighted. Then we stopped." [48]

Mies wrote the letter and the school was closed.

Closing the Bauhaus reflected, in microcosm, what was happening elsewhere in Germany—the systematic elimination of individual freedom. As soon as he assumed power in 1933, Hitler moved to exclude certain groups of individuals from positions of power or influence: from public office, civil service, teaching positions, journalism and the theatre. In 1935 these actions were followed by even more repressive "legal" measures, the Nuremberg Laws, which formally deprived Jews as well as certain other individuals and groups of their civil rights. At a very practical level, this meant that clients were discouraged or openly prevented from retaining architects and designers identified with the Modern Movement. In Mies's case, he was to receive only four commissions between 1933 and 1938: a

104. *Model of a four-bedroom house designed by Howard Dearstyne under Mies at the Berlin Bauhaus, 1932–33.*

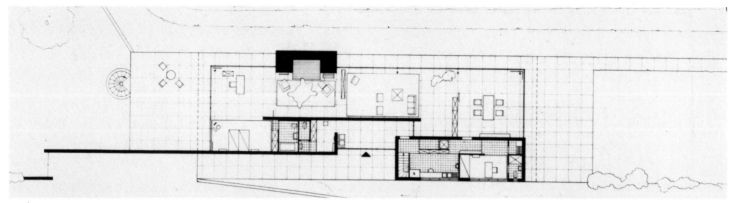

105. In September 1933, a few students from the Berlin Bauhaus went to Lugano, Switzerland, to continue their architectural studies with Mies and Reich. This house on a plateau was designed by Howard Dearstyne in Lugano.

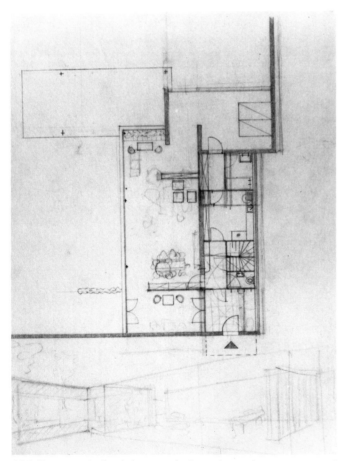

106. Dearstyne's sketch for a one-bedroom house showing suggested changes, and a freehand perspective by Mies, 1931.

factory building for the silk industry, Krefeld, Germany (1932–33); the Ulrich Lange house, Krefeld, Germany (1935); the Hubbe house, Magdeburg, Germany (1935); and an Administration Building for the silk industry, Krefeld, Germany (1937). Only two of these resulted in completed buildings.[49] Mies survived on royalties from the sale of his metal furniture which, despite an official attitude against it, continued to be used in business and professional offices. Later, even this source of income was threatened by a series of patent infringements by other manufacturers. In 1937 Mies initiated several lawsuits to protect his rights. After years of litigation which continued during World War II, the judgment went against Mies.[50] Without a doubt, the Third Reich's court's decision was influenced by the politics of the time and by the fact that in 1944 Mies had become a naturalized citizen of the United States of America.

The social, economic and political erosion which the Great Depression and National Socialism precipitated resulted in Mies's gradual isolation from the encouragement and financial support of clients. At the official level, his work was judged incompatible with the goals and values of the Third Reich. His competition entry for the German Pavilion at the International Exposition, Brussels (1934) was, according to one account, rejected by Hitler himself. Mies's other competition entry, the Reichsbank, Berlin (1933), was the only "modern" solution among the six finalists.

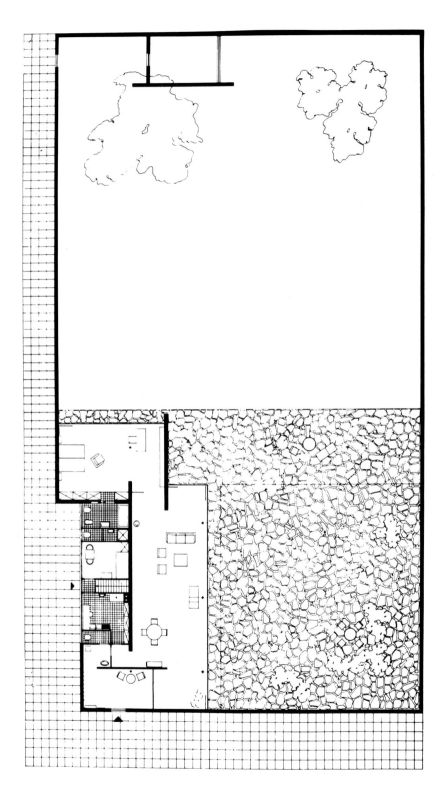

107. One of the problems Mies assigned his students at the Dessau Bauhaus was the design of a court house. This is Dearstyne's solution incorporating some changes and refinements suggested by Mies.

108. Mies's sketch of the changes he proposed for the entrance to Dearstyne's court house, 1931.

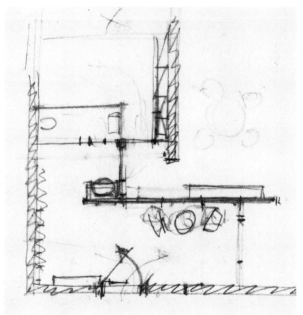

109, 110. Under Mies, Eduard Ludwig redesigned an existing department store in Dessau, Germany, 1932. The store and its proposed new facade.

That it was "modern" did not make it any more acceptable to the inept and politically motivated jurors.[51] It, too, was summarily rejected as being incompatible with the Third Reich's aesthetics.

Mies's solution was a simple, symmetrical, factory-like building of imposing scale and sublime monumentality. Its main lobby was a gently curved space 350 feet long by 50 feet wide and 30 feet tall. The exterior surfaces were devoid of ornamentation and consisted of alternating horizontal bands of masonry (?) and glass supported on the floor construction which cantilevered beyond the column face.

Though limited in his commissioned work, Mies used the time after the closing of the Bauhaus to study architectural problems which were of interest to him. The Barcelona Pavilion and the House for a Bachelor had suggested the possibility of urban residences which incorporated walled courts. As early as 1931 in a series of studies which lasted several years, he heightened the tension as well as the spatial ambiguity between inside and outside in a series of court-house projects. The enclosing walls define open courts and simultaneously imply and confirm the existence of space beyond the walled perimeter. All of this was accomplished with great subtlety. In so doing Mies enhanced our perception of and appreciation for space itself, enriching the total experience with the inclusion of sculpture and the landscape.

As the Third Reich's infatuation with nationalism gained momentum, it resulted in a boycott of the architects and designers of the Modern Movement. In spite of the deep affection he felt for his homeland, Mies was being forced to decide whether it was possible to stay in Germany and maintain his freedom of expression, to remain and pursue the path of accommodation, or to leave. In the end, there was only one real choice. Faced with the incompatibility of freedom of expression with life under National Socialism and the probability that he would be arrested,[52] Mies decided to leave.

In 1936 Dean Joseph Hudnut interviewed Mies in Berlin

111. *The factory which Mies rented to house the Bauhaus in Berlin, 1932.*

112. *Lilly Reich (seated) and Ludwig Hilberseimer (to her right) meeting with students on the morning when the Nazis closed the Berlin Bauhaus, April 11, 1933.*

113. Silk Factory, Krefeld, Germany, 1932–33.

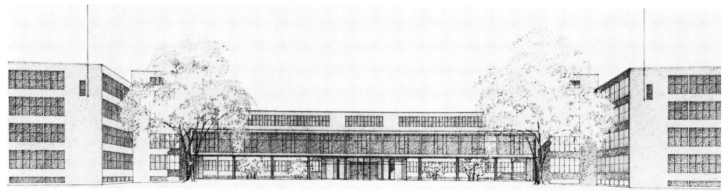

114. Silk Industry Administration Building, Krefeld, Germany, 1937. Exterior perspective.

115. Silk Industry Administration Building. Model.

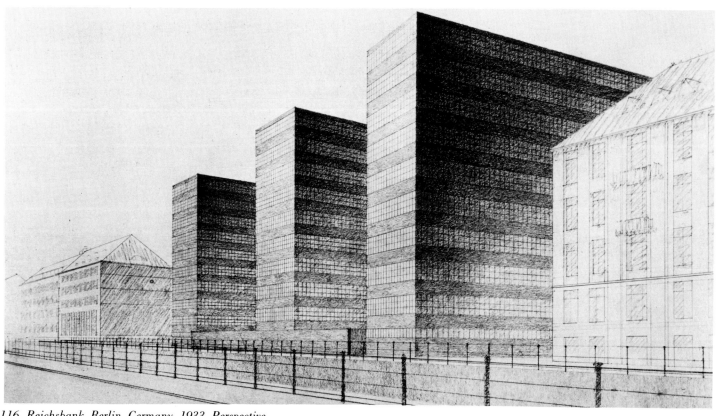

116. Reichsbank, Berlin, Germany, 1933. Perspective.

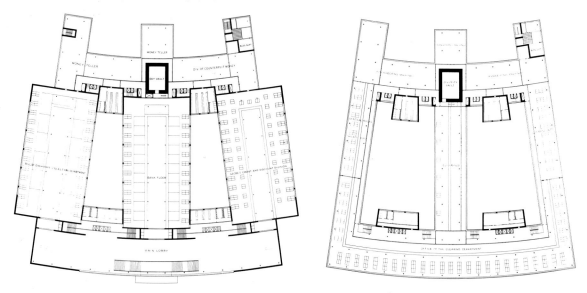

117, 118. Reichsbank. Ground floor and typical floor plans.

100

119. Reichsbank. Elevation.

120. Reichsbank. Model.

101

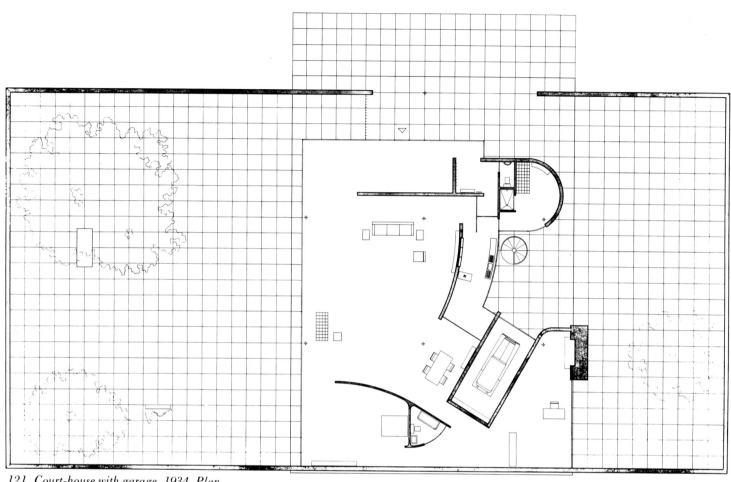

121. Court-house with garage, 1934. Plan.

for the professorship of design at Harvard University's College of Architecture. Mies was not appointed, but Gropius, also under consideration, was.[53] Later, at Philip Johnson's suggestion, Mr. and Mrs. Stanley Resor invited Mies to the United States in 1937 to look at the Jackson Hole, Wyoming, site for a guest house they proposed to have him design.[54] Hoping that life in the United States would offer Mies the freedom in which he needed to work, he sailed for America to accept the commission.

During his visit to the States, John A. Holabird, a prominent Chicago architect and chairman of the search committee for a director of architecture at Armour (later Illinois) Institute of Technology, invited Mies to Chicago to discuss his possible appointment to that position.[55] Mies was offered the directorship, accepted the position, then returned to Germany to quickly settle his affairs, and quietly set sail again for America in early 1938. Lilly Reich did not accompany him back to the States nor did any members of his family. In 1939 Reich did visit Mies in New York City and Chicago[56] but returned to Germany for personal reasons.[57] By returning to Germany, Reich was able to preserve Mies's drawings and represent him in the litigation involving patent infringement in the manufacture of his metal furniture. He would never see her again; she died of cancer in 1947,[58] and with her death ended one of the century's most creative collaborations in architecture.

122. House with three courts, 1934. Plan and elevation.

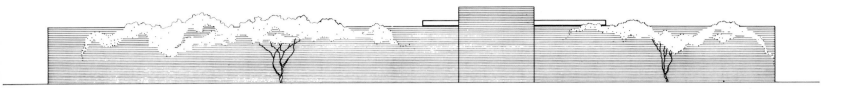

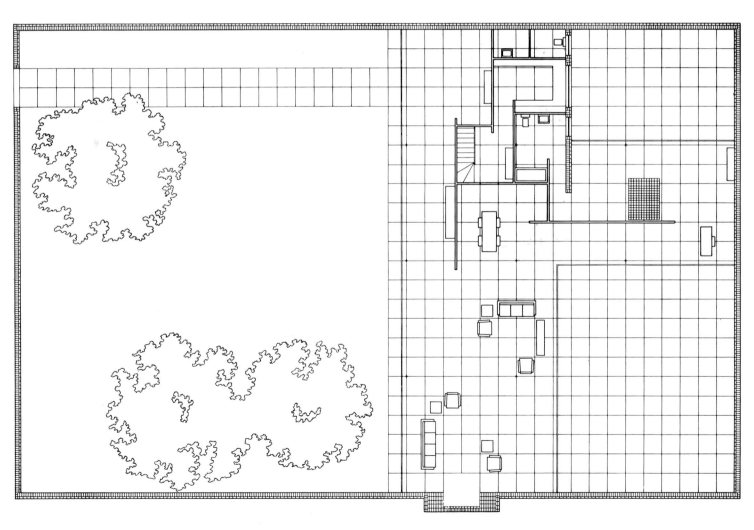

103

123. Resor house, Jackson Hole, Wyoming, 1937–38. Model on a different site.

1 George Nelson, "Architects of Europe today . . . van der Rohe, Germany," *Pencil Points* 16 (September 1935): 460.

2 Ludwig Glaeser, *Ludwig Mies van der Rohe: Furniture and Furniture Drawings: from the Design Collection and the Mies van der Rohe Archive* (New York: Museum of Modern Art, 1977), 7.

3 Ibid. According to Glaeser, there was a rather heated debate at the *Werkbund's* 1914 meeting in Cologne concerning whether designers should develop furniture prototypes for mass production or create unique masterpieces.

4 Ibid., 13.

5 Philip Johnson, *Mies van der Rohe* (New York: Museum of Modern Art, 1953), 198.

6 Glaeser, *Ludwig Mies van der Rohe: Furniture and Furniture Drawings.* 9.

7 Ibid.

8 Ibid., 8–9. While Glaeser does not reject the idea that tubular steel furniture was a direct outgrowth of its time, he has speculated that the development of the cantilevered chair was as much a symbolic event as it was a technological feat.

9 *Bau und Wohnung: die Bauten der Weissenhofsiedlung in Stuttgart errichtet 1927* (Stuttgart: F. Wedekind, 1927), 7.

10 Johnson, *Mies van der Rohe,* 194.

11 Lilly Reich never married. It was, however, customary in Germany at this time to address a professional woman whether single or married as Frau. It was a title of courtesy rather than an indication of marital status.

12 Glaeser, *Ludwig Mies van der Rohe: Furniture and Furniture Drawings,* 13.

13 While Reich maintained a residence separate from Mies's, they became all but inseparable. In addition, she took over management of Mies's household (including the staff) and entertained his daughters during their visits to Berlin to see their father. During these visits the children stayed with her in her apartment as Mies did not have a guest room in his. (This according to Georgia van der Rohe.) Mies never publicly defined their relationship. It was not the sort of announcement someone as reticent as Mies could have made or that most Berliners would have accepted if he had done so. For all concerned it seemed better that Mies and Reich appear only as business partners.

14 Personal communication with Howard Dearstyne.

15 Joan Campbell, *The German Werkbund: The Politics of Reform in the Applied Arts* (Princeton: Princeton University Press, 1978), 153.

16 "Die neue Zeit: Schlussworte des Referats Mies van der Rohe auf der Wiener Tagung des deutschen Werkbundes," *Die Form* 5hft1 (August 1, 1930): 406.

17 Ludwig Hilberseimer, "Eine Würdigung des Projektes Mies van der Rohe für die Umbauung des Alexanderplatzes," *Das Neue Berlin* hft 2 (February 1929): 39–41.

18 "6 Students talk with Mies," *North Carolina University State College of Agriculture and Engineering, School of Design Student Publication* 2 (Spring 1952): 23.

19 H. T. Cadbury-Brown, "Ludwig Mies van der Rohe: An Address of Appreciation," *Architecture Association Journal* 75 (July 1959): 31.

20 Ludwig Glaeser, *Mies van der Rohe: The Barcelona Pavilion 50th Anniversary* (New York: Museum of Modern Art—Mies van der Rohe Archive, 1979), (1.)

21 "Mies Speaks.," *Architectural Review,* 451.

22 Ibid.

23 "6 Students Talk with Mies," 28.

24 Ludwig Mies van der Rohe, "Baukunst und Zeitwille," *Der Querschnitt* 4 (1924): 31.

25 Glaeser, *Mies van der Rohe: The Barcelona Pavilion,* (1.)

26 Juan Pablo Bonta, *An Anatomy of Architectural Interpretation: A Semiotic Review of the Criticism of Mies van der Rohe's Barcelona Pavilion* (Barcelona: Gustavo Gili, 1975), 57–58.

27 Johnson, *Mies van der Rohe,* 199.

28 Walther Genzmer, "Der Deutsche Reichspavillon auf der Internationalen Ausstellung, Barcelona," *Die Baugilde* 11 (1929): 1654–57.

29 Helen Appleton Read, "Germany at the Barcelona World's Fair," *Arts* 16 (October 1929): 112–13.

30 Cadbury-Brown, "Ludwig Mies van der Rohe," 29.

31 "Die Bewohner des Hauses Tugendhat äussern sich," *Die Form* 6hft11 (November 15, 1931): 439.

32 Justus Bier, and Walter Riezler, "Kann Man im Haus Tugendhat wohnen?," *Die Form* 6hft10 (October 15, 1931): 393.

33 Ibid.

34 "Die Bewohner des Hauses Tugendhat äussern sich," 439.

35 Glaeser, *Ludwig Mies van der Rohe: Furniture and Furniture Drawings*, 10.

36 Ibid.

37 Henry-Russell Hitchcock, and Philip Johnson, *The International Style: Architecture Since 1922* (New York: Norton, 1932).

38 Glaeser, *Ludwig Mies van der Rohe: Furniture and Furniture Drawings*, 14.

39 Hans Maria Wingler, *The Bauhaus: Weimer, Dessau, Berlin, Chicago* translated by Wolfgang Jabs and Basil Gilbert. Edited by Joseph Stein (Cambridge: MIT Press, 1969), 10.

40 Ibid.

41 With Anderson Todd, a friend and professional associate of Mies's, Mies discussed the reasons for his appointment to the directorship of the Bauhaus. According to Todd, Mies felt that his organizational skills were what impressed the Dessau municipal authorities.

42 "Mies Speaks.," *Architectural Review*, 452.

43 Mies van der Rohe, "The End of the Bauhaus," *North Carolina University State College of Agriculture and Engineering, School of Design Publication*, 3 (Spring 1953): 17.

44 Wassily Kandinsky (1866–1944) was born in Russia. Prior to becoming a painter, he studied law in Moscow and, having passed his examinations, joined the faculty there in 1893. In 1896 he rejected another faculty appointment and began to study painting over the next few years with a variety of teachers. While he held no rigid views about form, he did develop a theory of harmony similar to that proposed in 1911 by Arnold Schönberg, the composer. He joined the Bauhaus's faculty in 1922 as a master responsible for the first term's required class in mural painting.

45 Mies van der Rohe, "The End of the Bauhaus," 18.

46 "Mies Speaks.," *Architectural Review*, 452.

47 Adolf Hitler, *Mein Kampf*, eine Abrechnung, von Adolf Hitler. . . (Munchen: F. Eher nachf., [1925–27] 1936), 337–38. This passage translated by Carol Dussere, Ph.D.

48 Mies van der Rohe, "The End of the Bauhaus," 18.

49 The factory building for the silk industry is not included on the list of Mies's buildings as published by Carter in *Mies van der Rohe at Work*. However, Alison and Peter Smithson documented its existence and illustrated it in their collection of essays: *Without Rhetoric: An Architectural Aesthetic 1955–1972* (London: Latimer New Dimensions, Ltd., 1973), 37.

50 Glaeser, *Ludwig Mies van der Rohe: Furniture and Furniture Drawings*, 14–15.

51 Sergius Ruegenberg, "Ludwig Mies van der Rohe (1886–1969)," *Deutsche Bauzeitung* 103 (September 1, 1969): 660.

52 According to Dearstyne, Mies's friends thought his arrest by the Nazis was imminent.

53 Franz Schulze, "How Chicago got Mies—and Harvard Didn't," *Inland Architect* 21 (May 1977): 23.

54 Peter Blake, *The Master Builders* (New York: Knopf, 1960), 213.

55 "Mies van der Rohe joins Armour Faculty," *Pencil Points* 19 (October 1938): Sup. 45.

56 Dearstyne arranged hotel accommodations for Mies and Reich during their stay in New York. He also took them on a tour of the World's Fair with which, he reported, they were unimpressed.

57 Personal communication with George Danforth, Mies's successor at IIT and close friend.

58 Mies was not insensitive to her plight in Europe. With the war's end, he sent her CARE packages on a regular basis until her death. He also sent CARE packages to his wife and daughters and to his brother, Ewald.

Page 106
124. Farnsworth house, Plano, Illinois, 1945–50.

CHAPTER IV: 1938-1958

Certainly there have been several of his [Mies's] contemporaries who have made great thunders as shakers and movers, in order to get the best out of their moment in time and place, but none of them have done all that he has done with his very special kind of surprisingly illuminating light; with a logic at the highest level of meaningful truth, with an intellect making its points so precisely that it develops a most exciting progression from fact to the inevitabilities of reason, and on to the exquisite balance of poetry. And so, if I were a native of Chicago, I would want him to know how very grateful my city is for his having lived here, and for being not only man fulfilling its greatest tradition, but also for being its architectural conscience.[1]

—John Entenza, 1966

It was predestination that Mies should have moved to Chicago and not Cambridge or New York; for it was in Chicago that he found a tradition of architectural expression, similar to his own, known as the Chicago School.[2] He was clearly aware that this school had emerged from the same technological roots and concern for structural expression as his own architecture. However, when asked if the Chicago School had been a direct influence on his work, he remarked somewhat dryly:

"I really don't know the Chicago School. You see, I never walk. I always take taxis back and forth to work. I rarely see the city. In 1912 when I was working in The Hague I first saw a drawing by Louis Sullivan of one of his buildings. It interested me. Before I came to Chicago I also knew about Frank Lloyd Wright and particularly about the Robie House."[3]

More to the point, when asked further about Sullivan and Wright, he responded:

". . . we would not do what Sullivan did. We see with different eyes, because it is a different time. Sullivan still believed in the facade. It was still the old architecture. He did not consider that just the structure could be enough. Now we would go on for our own time—and we would make architecture with the structure only. Likewise with Wright. He was different from Sullivan, and we for equal reasons are different from Wright."[4]

Beginning as early as 1879 with William Le Baron Jenny's (1832–1907) First Leiter Building and culminating in Louis Sullivan's (1856–1924) Carson Pirie Scott Store (1899–1904), architects working in Chicago had articulated and refined the steel skeleton as the structural system appropriate to the skyscraper. But for nearly three decades prior to Mies's arrival in Chicago, most architects there had either ignored or abandoned the accomplishments of their nineteenth-century predecessors. They chose "architectonic imperialism"[5] over the architecture of structural expression.

In 1938 at a black-tie dinner and reception, Mies was formally introduced to the Chicago architectural community. Frank Lloyd Wright did the honors. It would not be an exaggeration to claim that there was hostility between Wright and this audience. With justification, Wright believed that the architects of Chicago had abandoned Sullivan and had lost sight of the architectural principles inherent in his writings and his work. Concluding his introduction, he commented, "Now I give you Mies van der Rohe—God knows you need him!" and promptly left the banquet hall.[6]

Mies responded with what can best be described as a glowing tribute to Wright and his influence on European architects from 1910, when his work was first exhibited there. Alas, the translator (Mies delivered his remarks in German) was not equal to the occasion and soon floundered.

125. *Illinois Institute of Technology, Chicago, Illinois. Aerial perspective of the preliminary proposal for the campus, 1939.*

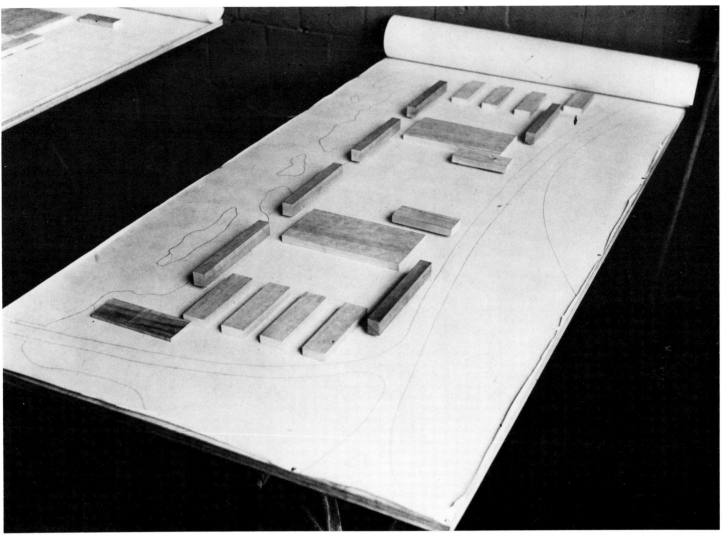

126. I.I.T. Model of the preliminary proposal for the campus.

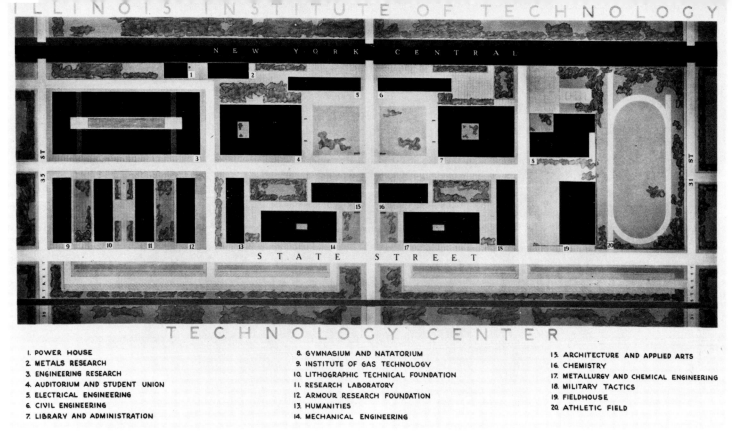

1. POWER HOUSE
2. METALS RESEARCH
3. ENGINEERING RESEARCH
4. AUDITORIUM AND STUDENT UNION
5. ELECTRICAL ENGINEERING
6. CIVIL ENGINEERING
7. LIBRARY AND ADMINISTRATION

8. GYMNASIUM AND NATATORIUM
9. INSTITUTE OF GAS TECHNOLOGY
10. LITHOGRAPHIC TECHNICAL FOUNDATION
11. RESEARCH LABORATORY
12. ARMOUR RESEARCH FOUNDATION
13. HUMANITIES
14. MECHANICAL ENGINEERING

15. ARCHITECTURE AND APPLIED ARTS
16. CHEMISTRY
17. METALLURGY AND CHEMICAL ENGINEERING
18. MILITARY TACTICS
19. FIELDHOUSE
20. ATHLETIC FIELD

127. *I.I.T. Final campus plan.*

In a state of trepidation, he translated Mies's tribute as: "Mies van der Rohe thanks you for inviting him here this evening."[7]

Mies had come to Chicago to be director of architecture at the Armour Institute of Technology. He was given a free hand to develop a new curriculum for architectural education. As that curriculum was refined over the next few years, it became apparent how influenced it was by Mies's experience at the Bauhaus. Indeed, Mies's first faculty appointments, Walter Peterhans and Ludwig Hilberseimer, were former teaching colleagues there.[8] With the curriculum which Gropius had instituted at the Bauhaus, there was to be logic and order in the sequence of learning experiences which Mies instituted at Armour.

As the curriculum evolved over the next twenty years during which he remained as director, it became clear that architectural education at Armour was not to be simply a transplanted version of Gropius' Bauhaus. Chicago was not Weimar, Dessau or Berlin. The new situation demanded a different approach.[9]

Mies articulated what this new curriculum was to be like at his inauguration in 1938 as director of architecture. Central to the curriculum was a primary concern for the acquisition of certain technical skills. This preoccupation addressed itself not only to the craft of architecture but also to the spiritual aspects of education. As Mies stated:

"All education must begin with the practical side of life.

Real education, however, must transcend this to mould the personality.

The first aim should be to equip the student with the knowledge and skill for practical life.

The second aim should be to develop his personality and to enable him to make the right use of this knowledge and skill.

Thus true education is concerned not only with practical goals but also with values.

By our practical aims we are bound to the specific structure

110

of our epoch. Our values, on the other hand, are rooted in the spiritual nature of men.

Our practical aims measure only our material progress. The values we profess reveal the level of our culture.

Different as practical aims and values are, they are nevertheless closely connected.

For to what else should our values be related if not to our aims in life?

Human existence is predicated on the two spheres together. Our aims assure us of our material life, our values make possible our spiritual life.

If this is true of all human activity where even the slightest question of value is involved, how especially is it true of the sphere of architecture.

In its simplest form architecture is rooted in entirely functional considerations, but it can reach up through all degrees of value to the highest sphere of spiritual existence, into the realm of pure art.

In organizing an architectural education system we must recognize this situation if we are to succeed in our efforts. We must fit the system to this reality. Any teaching of architecture must explain these relations and interrelations.

We must make clear, step by step, what things are possible,

128. I.I.T., 1939. Perspective of the proposed campus.

111

129, 131. Minerals and Metals Research Building, I.I.T., 1942–43.

necessary and significant.

If teaching has any purpose, it is to implant true insight and responsibility.

Education must lead us from irresponsible opinion to true responsible judgment.

It must lead us from chance and arbitrariness to rational clarity and intellectual order.

Therefore let us guide our students over the road of discipline from materials, through function, to creative work. Let us lead them into the healthy world of primitive building methods, where there was meaning in every stroke of an axe, expression in every bite of a chisel.

Where can we find greater structural clarity than in the wooden building of old? Where else can we find such unity of material, construction and form?

Here the wisdom of whole generations is stored.

What feeling for material and what power of expression there is in these buildings!

What warmth and beauty they have! They seem to be echoes of old songs.

And buildings of stone as well: what natural feeling they express!

What a clear understanding of the material! How surely it is joined!

What sense they had of where stone could and could not be used!

Where do we find such wealth of structure? Where more natural and healthy beauty?

How easily they laid beamed ceilings on those old stone walls and with what sensitive feeling they cut doorways through them!

What better examples could there be for young architects? Where else could they learn such simple and true crafts than from these unknown masters?

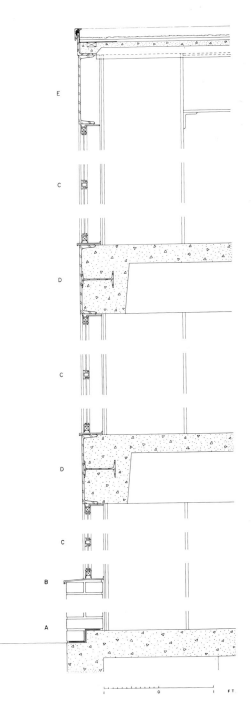

130. Minerals and Metals
Research Building, I.I.T. Exterior
details.

113

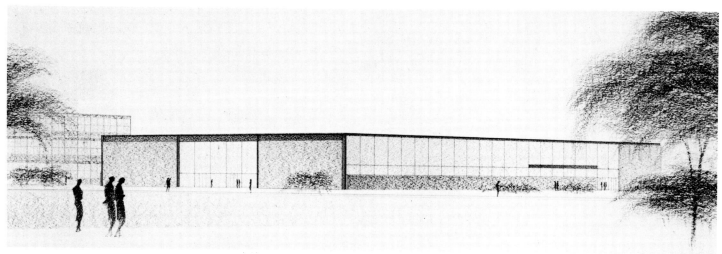

132. Library and Administration Building, I.I.T., 1944. Exterior perspective.

We can also learn from brick.

How sensible is this small handy shape, so useful for every purpose! What logic in its bonding, pattern and texture!

What richness in the simplest wall surface! But what discipline this material imposes!

Thus each material has its specific characteristics which we must understand if we want to use it.

This is not less true of steel and concrete. We must remember that everything depends on how we use a material, not on the material itself.

Also new materials are not necessarily superior. Each material is only what we make it.

We must be as familiar with the functions of our buildings as with our materials. We must analyze them and clarify them. We must learn, for example, what distinguishes a building to live in from other kinds of building.

We must learn what a building can be, and what it should be, and also what it must not be.

We shall examine one by one every function of a building and use it as a basis for form.

Just as we acquainted ourselves with materials and just as we must understand functions, we must become familiar with the psychological and spiritual factors of our day.

No cultural activity is possible otherwise; for we are dependent on the spirit of our time.

Therefore we must understand the motives and forces of our time and analyze their structure from three points of view: the material, the functional and the spiritual.

We must make clear in what respects our epoch differs from others and in what respects it is similar.

At this point the problem of technology of construction arises.

We shall be concerned with genuine problems—problems related to the value and purpose of our technology.

We shall show that technology not only promises greatness and power, but also involves dangers; that good and evil apply to it as to all human actions; that it is our task to make the right decision.

Every decision leads to a special kind of order.

Therefore we must make clear what principles of order are

114

possible and clarify them.

Let us recognize that the mechanistic principle of order overemphasizes the materialistic and functionalistic factors in life, since it fails to satisfy our feeling that means must be subsidiary to ends and our desire for dignity and value.

The idealistic principle of order, however, with its over-emphasis on the ideal and the formal, satisfies neither our interest in simple reality nor our practical sense.

So we shall emphasize the organic principle of order as a means of achieving the successful relationship of the parts to each other and to the whole.

And here we shall take our stand.

The long path from material through function to creative work has only a single goal: to create order out of the desperate confusion of our time.

We must have order, allocating to each thing its proper place and giving to each thing its due according to its nature.

We would do this so perfectly that the world of our creations will blossom from within.

We want no more; we can do no more.

Nothing can express the aim and meaning of our work better than the profound words of St. Augustine: "Beauty is the splendor of Truth." [10]

133. Mies with Frank Lloyd Wright at Taliesin, Wisconsin, 1937.

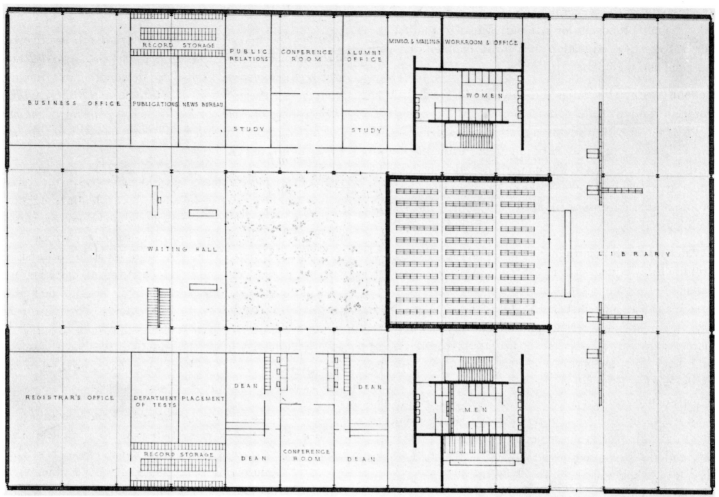

134. Library and Administration Building, I.I.T. Main floor plan.

In describing the general content and structure of his educational proposals for Armour, Mies, in reality, described his own education in a prose manner rich with lyricism and metaphor.

Teaching compelled Mies to clarify his ideas; and, in so doing, he and his faculty transmitted not a "Miesian style" but a way of solving problems or rather an "Order of Work" which began with the stern injunction: "Draw the known facts."[11] Because there was no preconception as to what a specific problem was to look like or how it was to be solved, problem solutions were induced rather than imposed by the faculty.

Given that there was a clear idea about architecture and architectural education, a student's course of study was consistent and cumulative. Nothing he or she learned in previous years was discarded. Taken as a whole, each experience and skill formed part of an integrated progression, the student not being asked to undertake some task or problem before they had acquired and refined the requisite skills. Architectural education was not seen as an exercise in self-expression for its own sake. The curriculum led toward a study of general principles and toward a concern for universal rather than special solutions. This attitude left students in a better position to deal with special cases than if they had approached each problem from a particular point of view.

Within two years of Mies's arrival, Armour merged with the Lewis Institute, another Chicago educational institution, to form the Illinois Institute of Technology (IIT). Dr. Henry Heald, the first president of IIT, asked Mies to prepare a master plan for the new campus and to undertake the design of the new facilities.[12] It was almost an unprecedented opportunity; not since Thomas Jefferson's University of Virginia had an architect been permitted to design an entire campus. But Mies's task was in some ways more complicated than Jefferson's, since unlike the virgin Charlottesville site, the IIT campus had to be painstakingly inserted into an already existing neighborhood. Mies understood the possibilities and the pitfalls the commission presented. Above all, he felt the campus should be unified:

"I firmly believe a campus must have unity. Allowing every building or group of buildings to be designed by a different architect is sometimes considered democratic, but from my point of view this is just an excuse to avoid the responsibility of accepting one clear idea. The only American campus worth the name was built by Thomas Jefferson at the University of Virginia."[13]

The IIT campus is located on Chicago's Southside, adjacent to what was a once-fashionable residential neighborhood, which by 1940 had become a slum. However, Heald and IIT's board of directors saw the new campus as a possibility for revitalizing the entire area. In cooperation with the Michael Reese Hospital and various other institutions in the vicinity which were then also beginning building programs, IIT began to acquire the land for a campus. Since over 3,000 individual parcels had to be assembled, acquisition was a long, slow process. Mies soon came to understand that he would have to think in terms of decades rather than years for the realization of his plan.

Mies's analysis of the problem suggested the use of a module or ordering device which would be flexible enough to accommodate classrooms, laboratories and offices. This repetitive module would also be economic and efficient in terms of construction. These conditions suggested the use of skeleton construction on the grounds of flexibility and economy, but only rarely had such a structure been clearly expressed. For Mies, "Only a clear expression of the structure could give us an architectural solution which would last."[14] When challenged that the earlier buildings would become outmoded, Mies responded:

"I was not afraid of that. The concept would not become outmoded for two reasons. It is radical and conservative at once. It is radical in accepting the scientific and technological driving and sustaining forces of our time. It has a scientific character, but it is not science. It uses technological means, but it is not technology. It is conservative as it is not only concerned with a purpose but also with a meaning,

117

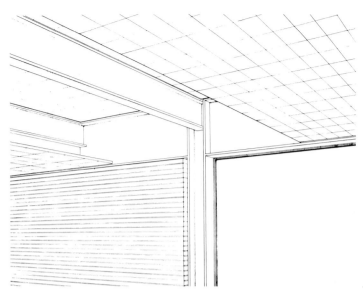

135. *Library and Administration Building, I.I.T. Interior perspective.*

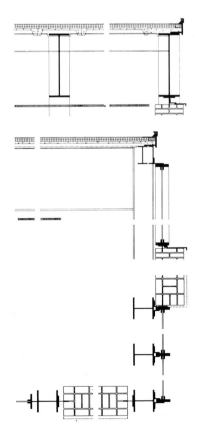

136. *Library and Administration Building, I.I.T. Vertical and horizontal sections.*

as it is not only concerned with a function but also with an expression. It is conservative as it is based on the eternal laws of architecture: Order, Space, Proportion."[15]

After a number of studies some of which, with their curvilinear street pattern, were almost suburban in character, Mies was brought to accept the existing Chicago gridiron plan. On to this grid of intersecting streets, he superimposed a three-dimensional module 24 feet by 24 feet by 12 feet. Initially, all building dimensions were to have been whole number multiples of 24 feet in plan and 12 feet in height. However, according to Mies:

"The Library and Administration Building and the Student Union confronted us with different problems. I wanted these two buildings in the center of the campus to have a more monumental character, an expression of dignity of a great institution. Could that be done with the same means? That was the real question."[16]

For these two buildings, the grid was enlarged by lengthening one side of the 24 foot square bay to 64 feet and increasing the ceiling height to 30 feet.

It is characteristic of many of Mies's preliminary campus designs as well as of the final one that the principal buildings are arranged symmetrically about an axis which runs across the short dimension of the site. However, the device of allowing individual buildings to relate asymmetrically to each other was to afford overlap (elision) between one building and the next. This strategy allowed Mies to create a series of open landscaped spaces of various sizes and by virtue of these "shifts" to combine the new buildings and the existing gridiron into a unified whole. In IIT there is never that sense of enclosure or containment which is so characteristic of the collegiate quadrangle. On the other hand, there is always a feeling of spatial continuum. In establishing an ordered relationship between the whole and its parts, Mies had realized St. Augustine's definition of order: "The disposition of equal and unequal things, attributing to each its place."

In the Minerals and Metals Research Building (1942–43),

118

the first of the structures built on the new campus, we sense, at once, the appropriateness of Mies's vision of the campus, his mastery of architecture and his understanding of order. The laboratory has an exposed skeletal structure of painted steel infilled, both inside and out, with either factory glazing or brick. As one critic wrote in 1943:

"It is of special interest to those who have followed the development of modern architecture, for it is the first executed work of Mies van der Rohe in this country. Like his earlier buildings in Europe, the laboratory is distinguished by the utmost simplicity in the handling of structure and materials."[17]

The material shortages and limitations which resulted from United States' entry into World War II brought all but war-related construction on the campus to a halt. However, war-time shortages had no direct influence on Mies's work. In developing the structural system for the campus buildings, he had already accepted the discipline of skeletal steel construction. Within this discipline, he had refined a new grammar whose vocabulary consisted of rolled angles, channels, I-beams, and H-columns. In so doing, he made a new language for architecture from the means which society and technology had placed at his disposal. Using a comparable linguistic analogy, he stated:

". . . language can be used for normal day to day purposes as prose. And if you are very good at that you may speak a wonderful prose. And if you are really good you can be a poet. But it is the same language and its characteristic is that it has all these possibilities."[18]

Mies spoke a fine prose which, in his project for the Library and Administration Building (1944), transcended to poetry. "Steel is joined to steel or steel to glass or brick," as Philip Johnson wrote, "with all the taste and skill that formerly went into the chiseling of a stone capital or the painting of a fresco."[19] The unfireproofed structure of the Library and Administration Building would have had all the clarity of a Gothic cathedral.

Writing of it in 1946, another critic commented:

"This building, like the [Minerals and Metals] Research Building, has that sensitivity of line and that precision, purity and sincerity of design in general which has placed its author among the world's handful of contemporary leaders in architecture, in spite of the small amount of work he has executed."[20]

As World War II ended, Mies emerged from the construction limbo imposed by the war as a major figure who would shape the course of American and world architecture in the second half of the twentieth century. His reputation was firmly established by a major exhibition of his work mounted at the Museum of Modern Art in New York in 1947. Philip Johnson wrote the monograph for this retrospective exhibition in which he examined the origins of Mies's ideas and the nature of his architecture. For many years, this monograph was the most complete and important documentation of Mies's work. It presented his work to an ever-increasing audience of admirers. In addition to the numerous photographs and drawings of his European work, Mies exhibited projects and works completed since his arrival in the United States. While some of this work, such as the classroom buildings and laboratories at IIT and the Museum for a Small City project (1942), had been published elsewhere, this exhibition offered the most complete picture of his architecture to date.

One senses from one of the contemporary reviews that the appeal of the Mies exhibition was to the intellect rather than the emotions. Thus in 1947, Peter Blake wrote:

". . . Mies appeals to an almost rarified type of intellect. . . . There is something quite terrifying in [his] work, a clarity and decisiveness of vision that brushes aside everything that is not brutally honest, and ends up with a monumental simplicity."[21]

While other reviews praised Mies's clarity of structure and purity of form, only Charles Eames saw that the exhibition's installation itself created a space which said, "This is what it's all about." The drawings, models, photographs, and furniture all worked together to create a rich environment. "By moving and turning within these simple elements," Eames observed, "one feels the impact of each

137. *Museum for a small city, 1942. Collage.*

new relationship."[22]

In a society in which technology and industrialization were closely identified with the more banal aspects of mass production particularly in the aftermath of a highly destructive war, Mies's work offered visible proof that these same forces could be made to embrace civilization, art, architecture and philosophy. Mies's architecture held a subconscious attraction to a nation and a culture infatuated with and repulsed by the immediate post-war effects of industrialization, by the proliferation of automobiles and other consumer goods. But for Mies, as he had stated to the *Werkbund* in 1930, the question was not "what" to build but rather "how" to build it. Technology and industrialization were merely a means to an end: the slow unfolding of the inner structure of the time.[23]

In addition to introducing Mies's work to a larger public, the Museum of Modern Art exhibition provided viewers with an opportunity to study his drawings firsthand. As with his earlier renderings, Mies infused these later drawings with qualities which allowed them to be appreciated not only as representations of his buildings but also as works of art in themselves. In their rich chiaroscuro and

subtle textures, the charcoal and conté-crayon perspectives are worthy of any master. It was, however, in his use of collage that Mies was to achieve his most important breakthrough in terms of representing his concept of space two dimensionally.

In the 1930's Mies had combined collage with more traditional constructed perspectives in order to represent the court-house projects. Later in the more abstract collages of the Resor house, Mies was able to represent the spatial qualities of his work. The collages are as refined and considered as any of his buildings. They have about them that economy of line one can find in a painting by Paul Klee (1879–1940) and the spatial richness of a collage by Georges Braque (1882–1963). Mies evoked the feeling of three-dimensional space with absolute economy of two-dimensional means.

During preparations for the exhibition of his work at the Museum of Modern Art, Mies accepted the commission for a small house which was destined to be the clearest expression of his ideas about space and structure. This was the Farnsworth house (1945–50), which was to prove to be his most controversial building. The client, Dr. Edith Farnsworth (1904–77), was an intelligent and sensitive physician and a member of Northwestern University's Medical School faculty and a personal friend of Mies's when she asked him to design a weekend house.[24] Whether or not her decision was motivated by a desire that this building make an important contribution to modern architecture, the impact of the Farnsworth house—on an understanding of architectural space as defined and articulated by Mies—cannot be overestimated however much it was (and is) discussed and debated.

The site which Dr. Farnsworth purchased lies along the Fox River about sixty miles west of Chicago near the town of Plano. It was far enough removed from the city so that she could escape the pressures of her work, if only on weekends, and enjoy the pleasure of an unspoiled sky and the seasonal variety and richness of the native landscape. The site is virtually flat and, because of its proximity to the river, lies within a flood plain. A thin line of trees along the bank defines the river. Between them and a denser grove of trees to the north and east is a smooth, grassy meadow reminiscent of the Illinois prairie.

For several years, Mies produced no definitive sketches of the house. He waited patiently, like a chessmaster contemplating his next move, for his ideas to crystallize. Such creative inactivity was characteristic of his approach to problem solving. It was worth the wait in the case of the Farnsworth house for with it, as with the Tugendhat house, Mies radically changed the nature of domestic architecture. In the Farnsworth house, with its simple program and isolated site, Mies was able to liberate the structure as he had never done before.

The house consists of roof and floor planes supported on eight exposed steel H-columns. It is enclosed by sheets of plate glass which extend from floor to ceiling and from column to column. Into this enclosed space, which is fifty-five feet long and twenty-eight feet deep, Mies was to place only two fixed elements. The larger of the two, the service core, contains the kitchen, two bathrooms, a space for mechanical equipment and the fireplace. By its asym-

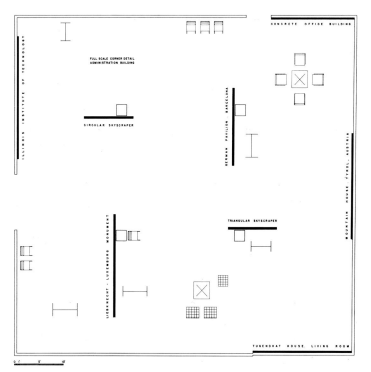

138. Plan of the exhibition of Mies's work at the Museum of Modern Art, New York, 1947.

139. Farnsworth house, Plano, Illinois, 1945–50. View of construction.

140. Farnsworth house. Plan.

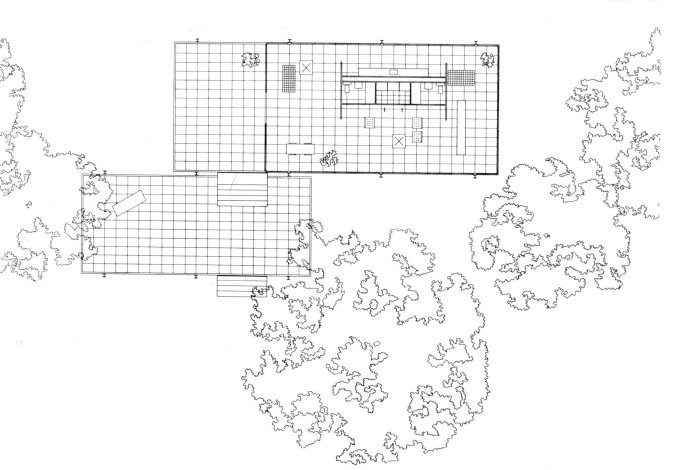

141. *Farnsworth house.*

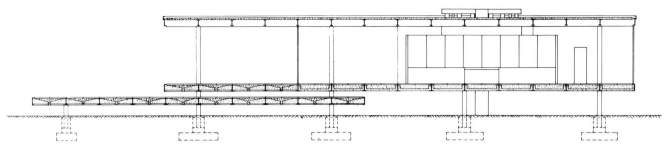

142. Farnsworth house. Longitudinal section.

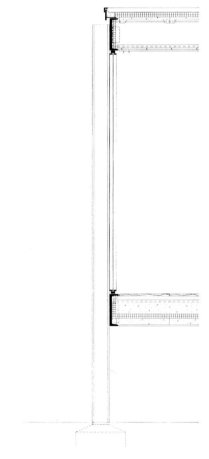

143. Farnsworth house. Exterior details.

metrical placement in the space, this core defines areas for living, dining and sleeping, while the other element, the wardrobe unit, screens the living from the sleeping area and vice versa.

Because the site is periodically subjected to flooding, Mies elevated the floor of the house five feet three inches above grade. While the prosaic result of this is protection of the living volume from inundation, the poetic effect is clearly a lightness and a sense of space only hinted at in his earlier work. Space can be said to flow under and over as well as through the house. Mies further heightened our awareness of the existence of architectural space by cantilevering the roof and floor planes beyond the columns at either end of the structure. This suspended effect was augmented by locating the living volume asymmetrically on the raised floor plane, and by placing an elevated terrace midway between the ground and the plane of the floor.

As in his earlier work, the placement of furniture in the Farnsworth house was of architectural significance and importance. Functional and aesthetic requirements were carefully balanced in this arrangement so that the exact location of furniture, as with other details, reinforced the idea of the house as a defined enclosure within a continuum. With subtlety and sophistication, beds, chairs and tables served as counterpoints to the fixed elements in the plan animating the total composition and enhancing the total spatial and architectural experience.

124

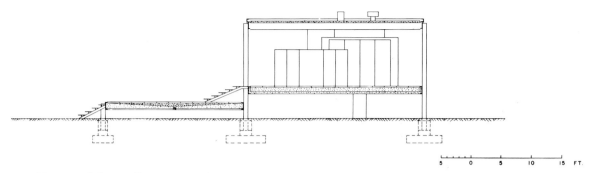

144. Farnsworth house. Transverse section.

Proportions, construction details, finishes and colors were as carefully considered by Mies as the placement of furniture. No formula or mathematical relationship forms the basis for the proportions; they were as much a response to the materials and the methods of fabrication and assembly as they are the result of what was satisfying to the eye and pleasing to the intellect.

The finishes are simple, muted, understated throughout. The floor is paved with slabs of Roman travertine, while the core is clad in Primavera wood panels. These materials are offset by a wardrobe of teak and curtains of natural Shantung silk. The exposed steel structure was carefully painted white after sandblasting, so that the resultant finish appears sprayed rather than brushed. Everywhere the sensitive and discerning eye of a master craftsman has seen that no element, no detail, distracts from an appreciation of the house as an artifact which is integral with its environment.

The Farnsworth house is Mies's summary statement of those spatial and architectural concerns he first realized in the Barcelona Pavilion, and which he further developed in the Tugendhat house and the House for a Bachelor. However, contained in what is a pure expression of its age is another vision, that of a transparent house in a verdant landscape. Suspended between earth and sky it is as appealing to the spirit as Schinkel's architecture or the paintings of his Romantic contemporary, Caspar David Friedrich (1774–1840). Arguably, in the Farnsworth house, Mies

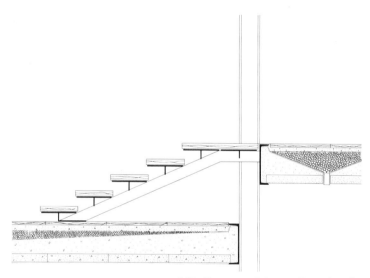

145. Farnsworth house. Stair details.

146. Farnsworth house. Exterior details.

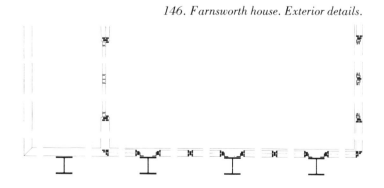

most clearly reveals his understanding of technology as an ideal one, perhaps even a Romantic one. Despite the clear expression of structure and careful articulation of means, technic and technique disappear. What remains is an untouched landscape.

Dr. Farnsworth, unhappy about the cost of such clarity and perfection, sued Mies for breach of contract—and lost.[25] The courtroom experience was painful and acrimonious for each of them. Although Mies's reputation remained intact, Dr. Farnsworth, who had agreed to all the change orders which had increased the cost of the house, was bitter and chose to vent her disappointment in a more public forum than a courtroom. She agreed to an interview with Elizabeth Gordon, editor of *House Beautiful* magazine. Gordon used the opportunity to compose a diatribe against modern architecture in general and against Mies and others specifically. Her attack, entitled "The Threat to the Next America," appears to have been motivated by an hysteria associated with McCarthyism when communists were thought to be everywhere and their influence complete and pernicious. Foreign-born individuals were immediately suspect because they were not native Americans. Gordon couched her arguments in terms of "comfort," "the need for individual expression" and "functional lines." To these qualities she added the requirement that they be "home grown."[26] "I have talked to a highly intelligent, now disillusioned, woman," wrote Gordon, "who spent more than $70,000 building a 1-room house that is nothing but a glass cage on stilts."[27]

Gordon's reservations about the house found some reflection in the professional press. For example Reyner Banham, architectural critic and historian, commented in 1981 when the American Institute of Architects awarded the Farnsworth house its prestigious "25-Year Award":

"The building has all the virtues—and we'll say nothing about the vices—of a particular concept of architecture driven to its extreme limits, and, therefore, a kind of landmark demonstration of what architecture could do. Like many extreme statements, it was made at the beginning rather than the end of the period it represents, and it left other architects little to do except to try to make even more perfect that which was already perfected."[28]

Craig Ellwood, a Miesian architect and member of the awards jury, proffered a totally different view: "All we need to do is compare the Farnsworth house with the nonsense we now call architecture. The truth about truth is it *is*."[29]

The Farnsworth house has stood the test of time and the judgment of history. Its beauty has come to be appreciated because it appeals to the senses, to the intellect, to the spirit. As James Marston Fitch wrote in 1963:

"To acclaim Mies for the monumental purity of his forms and yet to deplore their malfunction in some pragmatic details, is rather like praising the sea for being blue while chiding it for being salty, or admiring the tiger for the beauty of his coat while urging him to become a vegetarian."[30]

If, as Fitch suggests, critics were uncertain as to their expectations of Mies's work, they were also unclear as to the importance of the Farnsworth house and its relationship to the only other house from the same period to which it is often compared, the residence of Philip Johnson designed for himself in New Canaan, Connecticut (1949).

Shortly after completion of his residence, Johnson acknowledged his debt to Mies; at the same time he pointed out where and how he thought his approach to architecture differed from Mies's.[31] However, critics generally ignored Johnson's assertions. It was perceived that these two glass houses were similar if not exactly the same. The critics' confusion was understandable; for on the surface, at least, both residences seem the same. Both are simple, large "rooms" enclosed with sheets of plate glass; in each various domestic functions are defined by objects including furniture, not with walls; and their exposed steel structures were assembled from standard rolled shapes.

As Kenneth Frampton pointed out, in Johnson's and Mies's approach to the expression and articulation of structure

147. Johnson residence, New Canaan, Connecticut. Philip Johnson, 1949.

148. Johnson residence. Plan.

149. Johnson residence. Construction details.

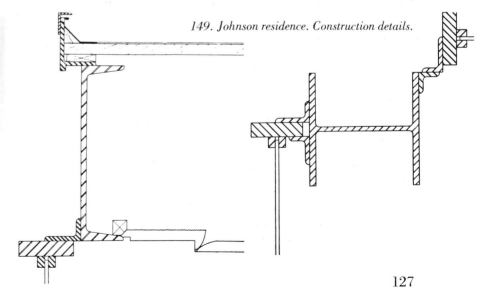

lies the essential difference between these two houses. Johnson's decision to place the columns immediately behind the enclosing glass skin results in "suppression" of the structure.[32] The taut skin of Johnson's residence, unanimated by shadows from the columns, defines a finite spatial volume, a prism. By placing the house directly on the ground and confining roof and floor planes within column lines, Johnson further reinforced the concept of a limited, defined space.

Mies's approach was just the opposite of Johnson's. At the Farnsworth house the glass skin passes behind the columns which assert their existence by this subtle articulation. And the living spaces and covered and uncovered terraces hover above the ground. Further, roof and floor planes cantilever beyond column lines so that the spatial experience of the Farnsworth house is an infinite not a finite one.

Sometime in 1946 during the early stages of the Farnsworth commission, Mies met Herbert Greenwald (1915–59). This meeting and their subsequent friendship was to have a profound and lasting impact on American urban architecture. Despite the thirty year difference in their ages, they had much in common. They shared a deep interest in philosophy, which Greenwald had studied at the University of Chicago prior to becoming a builder and real estate developer. In their respective ways they were idealists. Greenwald was interested in more than just making a profit from his real estate ventures; he wanted to create the finest architecture within the framework of twentieth-century technology and the economic realities of construction and land development costs.

Their initial joint endeavor, the Promontory Apartments (1946–49) on Chicago's Southside, was Mies's first realized high-rise structure. Originally it was designed as a steel frame building enclosed within a glass curtain wall, but economic considerations necessitated the substitution of reinforced concrete for steel. Conceived as an exposed skeleton filled with operating windows and brick spandrels, the exterior of the building is noteworthy for its simplicity

and restraint. The sole expressive element is the subtle reduction in the depth of the columns, which step back at three points on the facade as the load diminishes. In this way the Promontory Apartments combine the structural clarity of Sullivan's Carson Pirie Scott store and subtle structural refinement of a Gothic cathedral.

The virtues and accomplishments of the Promontory Apartments were quickly overshadowed by Mies's next two buildings for Greenwald, the 860 and 880 Lake Shore Drive Apartments (1948–51) on Chicago's Northside. These were the first high-rise apartments in the world constructed almost solely in glass and steel, and they ushered in a new age of architecture. As the Farnsworth house has done for the private dwelling, 860 and 880 (as they were more familiarly known) established a new standard of excellence for the apartment building. On a per-square-foot basis and allowing for inflation, 860 and 880 were only slightly more expensive to construct than the Promontory Apartments. At $10.38 and $8.55 per square foot respectively,[33] the cost of these three buildings was 5 to 10 pecent less than for conventional apartment construction in Chicago.[34]

Precision and refinement are everywhere evident, from the careful placement of the buildings on the trapezoid-shaped site to the details of the skin and the proportioning and articulation of the structure. It is through the details that the nature and idea of the building's structure is revealed on many levels.

The Chicago building code did not allow construction of an exposed, unfireproof, steel building more than one story in height. Mies was, therefore, faced with the problem of fireproofing the elements of the structure and at the same time expressing the nature of the material from which the structure was formed. As he had done for the IIT campus, Mies developed his vocabulary from standard rolled steel sections: I-beams, angles and plates were welded together to form the exterior skin, the framework to which windows were attached and the formwork for the concrete fireproofing. It is an organic approach to detailing; not only do the

129

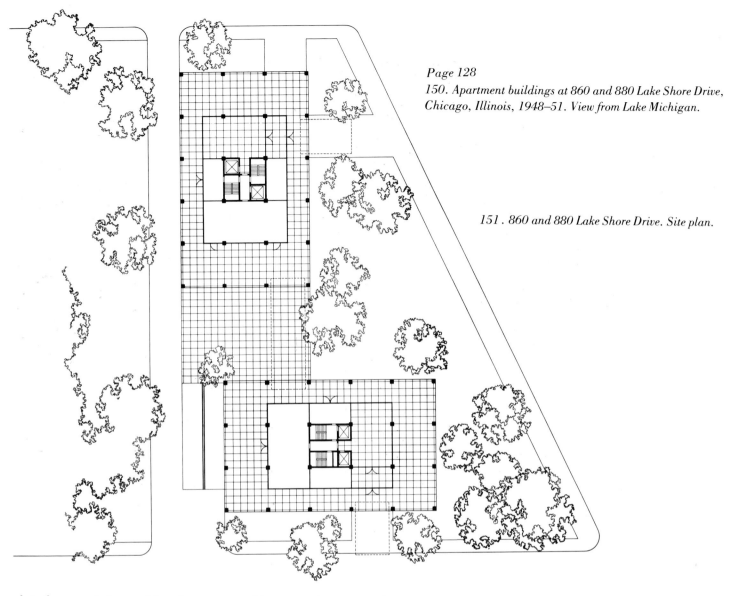

Page 128
150. Apartment buildings at 860 and 880 Lake Shore Drive, Chicago, Illinois, 1948–51. View from Lake Michigan.

151. 860 and 880 Lake Shore Drive. Site plan.

details reveal the architect's conceptual/structural intention, but they clearly express the technological means by which they were achieved.

The addition of I-beams to the steel plates which cover the columns caused a certain amount of critical comment at the time. Since the window mullions, at five-foot three-inch centers, were mounted on top of plates covering the columns, the windows adjacent to the columns are narrower than those in the center of the bays. This A-B-B-A rhythm is unique among Mies's tall buildings, and the visual result is subtle and satisfying. Through the play of

light and shadow created by the counterpoint of these projecting I-beams, an intermediate series of proportions and rhythms are developed. At the same time, the mullions signify the phenomenon of the structure if not its reality. To some critics the applied and apparently functionless I-beams were decoration. In an interview Mies offered the following explanation as to the real reason for these I-beams.

"... first I am going to tell you the real reason for those mullions, and then I am going to tell you a good reason by itself. It was very important to preserve and extend the rhythm which the mullions set up on the rest of the building.

152. *860 Lake Shore Drive. View of the lobby.*

We looked at it on the model without the steel section [I-beams] attached to the corner columns and it did not look right. That is the real *reason. Now the other reason is that the steel section was needed to stiffen the plate which covers the corner column so this plate would not ripple, and also we needed it for strength when the sections were hoisted into place. Now, of course, that's a very good reason—but the other one is the* real *reason."*[35]

The question of applied decoration or implied structure did not concern Frank Lloyd Wright, who dismissed the buildings as "flat-chested architecture!"[36] For Wright, Mies's

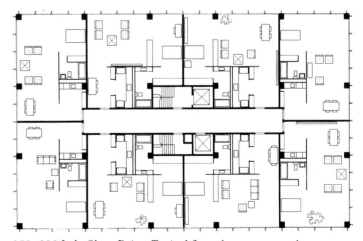

153. *880 Lake Shore Drive. Typical floor plans as proposed.*

131

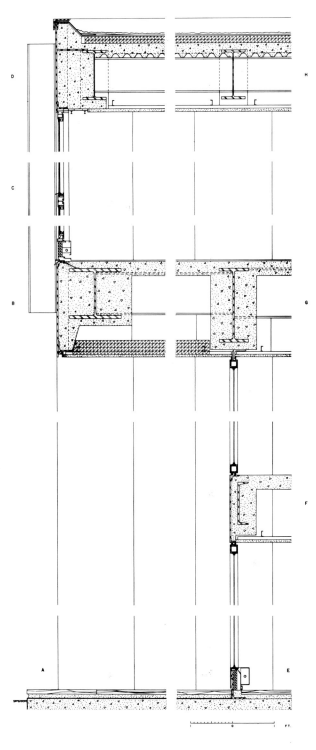

154. 860 and 880 Lake Shore Drive. Exterior details.

work in the United States left undeveloped the promise, the freedom and invention, of his European projects and buildings. As early as 1944, Wright expressed his disappointment and displeasure with the direction Mies's work was taking. Shortly after the presentation drawings for IIT's Library and Administration Building were completed, Wright visited Mies at the department of architecture then housed in an attic of the Chicago Art Institute. According to Bernard Goodman, one of Mies's students, who was present during Wright's visit, Wright studied the drawings for what seemed like several hours. Then he announced: "You know what you've done? You have invented a new classicism." His pronouncement did not invite discussion, and Wright left the studio without uttering another word. [37] In Mies, Wright wanted to find a disciple; it was a blind spot which, often as not, colored his judgment. What Wright found was a peer. Unwilling or unable to share the public attention, Wright dismissed both Mies and his work. What Wright could not see was that American technology offered Mies new possibilities as well as placing new (and different) restrictions on him.

Originally, individual apartment plans for 860 and 880 owed much to the Farnsworth house. Mies proposed using the placement of a core containing a kitchen and bathroom to define other spaces for living, dining and sleeping. Greenwald appreciated the quality of space which resulted but feared prospective tenants might be dismayed by such an uncompromising spatial statement. So Mies designed more conventional plans which are light, open and eminently habitable, though less spatially exciting.

860 and 880 were not air-conditioned, but subsequent apartment buildings that Mies designed for Greenwald were. Because both heat loss and heat gain occur on the exterior surfaces of the building, it was logical to heat and cool them along the perimeter. A new skin applied to the structure, rather than integral with it, was developed. Such a skin had to be deep enough to contain the pipes which supplied the individual air-conditioning units. It also had to be lightweight. Further, construction economics necessitated returning to reinforced concrete for the structure.

132

The column and flat-slab structure Mies used in these subsequent apartments had several advantages, not the least of which was the resulting finished floor and ceiling surfaces once the forms were removed. But how should such a structure be enclosed and with what material? In the case of a steel structure, steel was an obvious and logical choice. Unlike steel, however, reinforced concrete suggests no vocabulary of shapes: it is a plastic material capable of assuming almost any cast shape. In the end, however, aluminum proved the best choice for standard skin. Since it is lightweight, it can also be easily extruded into a variety of shapes. It was economical, and, if anodized, did not require painting as steel did.[38]

The inclusion of air-conditioning, coupled with the change in structural material, altered the physical and philosophical relationship between structure and skin in Mies's tall buildings. Architecture became, as Mies termed it, "skin and bones."[39] At 860 and 880, structure and skin were integral with each other and on the same plane. In subsequent concrete framed apartment buildings and in steel office buildings, the skin became a plane which passed in front of the structure without interruption or further articulation. This refinement in the relationship between structure and skin was the next logical step in the development of the Miesian Chicago School. Aside from fire protection revetment, the structural skeleton was enclosed in a light and transparent skin.

It was a characteristic of Mies's ideas about architecture and structure that they were visionary. Over thirty years elapsed between his Glass Skyscraper projects with their continuous skins of glass uninterrupted by columns and supported only along the outer edges of the floor slab, and the 900 and 910 Esplanade Apartments (1953–56) where he was able to realize such a "skin and bones" architecture. It had taken nearly three decades for technology to catch up with his vision.

It is characteristic of Mies's apartment plans that they are compact, yet spacious in their overall effect. He accomplished this by concentrating vertical services, elevators,

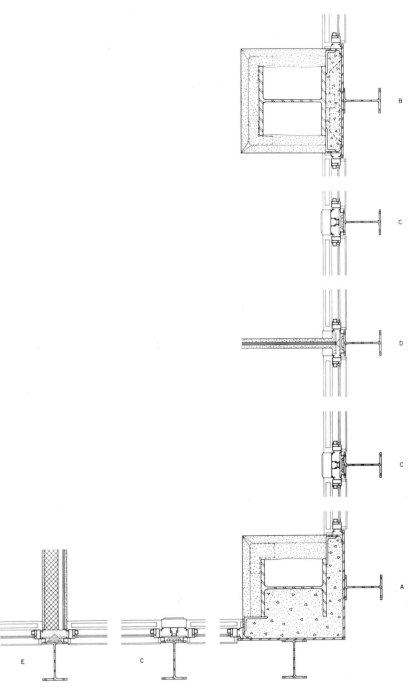

155. 860 and 880 Lake Shore Drive. Curtain wall details.

133

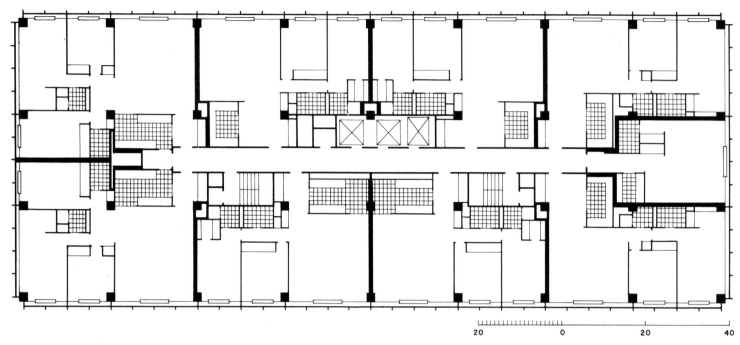

20 0 20 40

stairways and plumbing, in the center of each building and by locating kitchens and bathrooms away from the perimeter adjacent to these services. This approach made all glass exteriors possible, and the floor-to-ceiling windows incorporate space beyond this transparent membrane into individual apartments.

During the 1950's, nearly two-thirds of the work produced by Mies's office was under Greenwald's aegis. In addition to the Commonwealth Promenade and Esplanade Apartments, there were two urban redevelopment schemes; the larger and more important was Detroit's Lafayette Park (1955–63). Smaller in scope were the Colonnade and Pavilion Apartments (1958–60) which formed a part of Newark, New Jersey's, redevelopment. There were also three unrealized projects: a large-scale redevelopment for Chicago's Hyde Park neighborhood (1956); the Quadrangles Apartments, for Brooklyn (1957) and the Battery Park Apartments, for New York City (1957–58).

With each new apartment building, Mies advanced the state-of-the-art for glass curtain walls. The same was also true of the spatial planning for various apartment types

and for the inclusion, integration and refinement of air-conditioning systems. But Mies's greatest contribution was made, with his long-time friend and teaching colleague Ludwig Hilberseimer, in the area of urban redevelopment. With Greenwald, Mies and Hilberseimer proposed a major restructuring of Chicago's Hyde Park neighborhood. Streets were to be closed to through traffic or eliminated and replaced with pedestrian walkways and recreation space, thereby reducing the domination of the automobile within the city. Housing which was beyond rehabilitation was to have been replaced with new row houses and apartment buildings. The result—had it been realized—would have been an oasis of green spaces.

The Hyde Park plan served as excellent preparation for Greenwald, Mies and Hilberseimer's next work, Lafayette Park. Seventy-eight acres had been cleared as a large part of Detroit's urban renewal program. For the first time, Mies and Hilberseimer were presented with a site from which nearly all traces of the urban structure had been removed—only the existing street pattern remained. With Greenwald's support, they proposed that even this vestige of the

134

156. Commonwealth Promenade Apartment Building, Chicago, Illinois, 1953–56. Typical floor plan.

157. Hyde Park redevelopment, Chicago, Illinois, 1956. Model. New apartments, row houses, and court houses are shown dark.

135

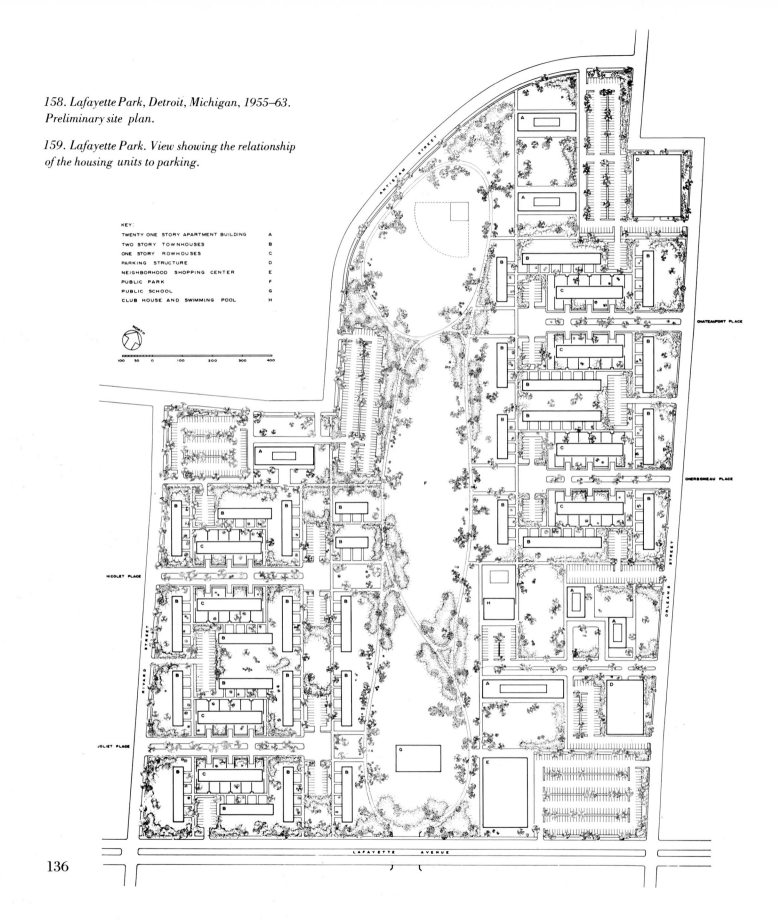

158. Lafayette Park, Detroit, Michigan, 1955–63. Preliminary site plan.

159. Lafayette Park. View showing the relationship of the housing units to parking.

KEY:

TWENTY ONE STORY APARTMENT BUILDING	A
TWO STORY TOWNHOUSES	B
ONE STORY ROWHOUSES	C
PARKING STRUCTURE	D
NEIGHBORHOOD SHOPPING CENTER	E
PUBLIC PARK	F
PUBLIC SCHOOL	G
CLUB HOUSE AND SWIMMING POOL	H

NORTH

100 50 0   100   200   300   400

160. *Lafayette Park.*

138

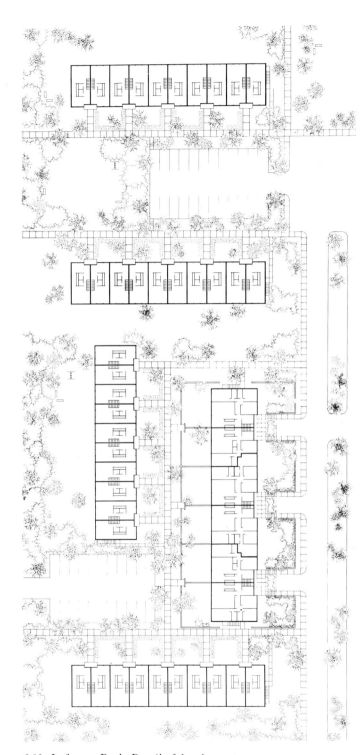

161. Lafayette Park. Detail of the plan.

nineteenth-century be eliminated.

What they arrived at was really a prototype for future urban redevelopment. The housing was a mixture of one-story court-houses, two-story row houses, and twenty-one-story apartment buildings. Through the center development ran a nineteen-acre park, accessible to pedestrians by a series of footpaths which ran through the housing units. The entire site was closed to through traffic; and in one final act of subjugation, surface parking for the automobile was provided four feet below the level of housing. In a few years, extensive landscaping by Alfred Caldwell (1903–), a teaching colleague at IIT, further softened what little intrusion the automobile made.

Two dimensionally, the arrangement of interconnecting green spaces recalls Mies's plan for the IIT campus, where buildings define but do not enclose exterior spaces. But the inclusion of tall apartment buildings with the lower row houses created a spatial richness not found at IIT. From a distance, Caldwell's landscaping creates the impression that the tall buildings exist amid a verdant, naturalistic landscape. With open spaces and landscaping, Lafayette Park provides the best of suburban living; and, because of its proximity to the center of Detroit, it offers the best of urban life within easy access to the city. While the history of urban renewal in the United States is littered with failures, Lafayette Park is one of the successes; one dehumanizing urban environment was not replaced with another. In Lafayette Park, with a shared vision and a common will, Mies, Hilberseimer, Caldwell and Greenwald achieved a working model for future urbanization. It is a new structure predicated on human values, disciplined but not dominated by the automobile.

In the thirteen years they worked together, Mies and Greenwald had ample reason to be proud of what they had accomplished and the quality of the buildings constructed. Both of their reputations were enhanced by the experience. On February 3, 1959, this nearly ideal working relationship came to an abrupt end. Herbert Greenwald was killed as the airplane in which he was a passenger crashed into

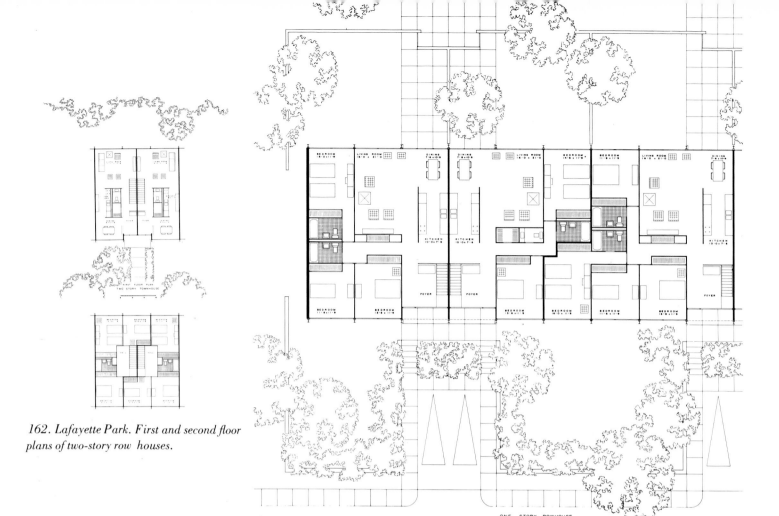

162. Lafayette Park. First and second floor plans of two-story row houses.

163. Lafayette Park. Floor plan of one-story row houses.

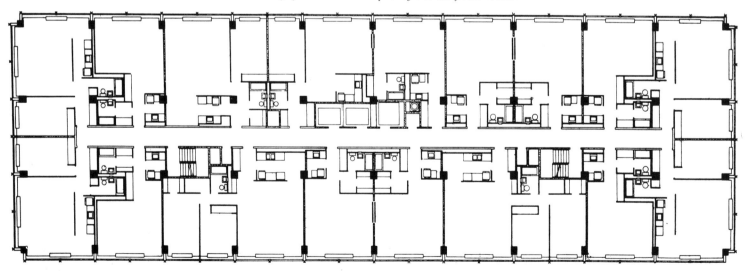

164. Pavilion Apartments, Lafayette Park, 1958. Floor plan.

140

New York City's East River. In summing up Greenwald's life, Mies stated, "Herbert Greenwald began with an idea of the social consequences of his work, along the way he also discovered that he was a very good business man."[40]

Commencing with the end of World War II and continuing to his retirement from the faculty in 1958, Mies's work on the IIT campus proceeded slowly but without serious interruption. It included construction of the following classroom and laboratory facilities: Alumni Memorial Hall (1945–46), Perlstein Hall (1945–46), Wishnick Hall (1945–46), Crown Hall (1950–56) and Siegel Hall (1955–57). Also constructed were the following facilities for research foundations related to IIT: for the Illinois Institute of Technology Research Institute, the Engineering Research Building (1944–46), the Mechanical Engineering Building (1950–52), the Physics-Electronics Research Building (1955–57), and the Metals Research Building (1955–58); laboratories for the Institute of Gas Technology (1945–50); and for the American Association of Railroads, an Administration Building (1948–50), a Mechanical Engineering Building (1948–53) and a Laboratory Building (1955–57). The following campus-related facilities were also constructed: a Boiler Plant (1945–50), St. Saviour Chapel (1949–52), Commons (1952–53), and three apartment buildings for faculty, staff and married students: Carmen (1951–53), Bailey (1952–55) and Cunningham (1952–55) Halls. In addition there were two other projects for the campus: a Student Union (1948) and a Dormitory and Fraternity House (1950).

While the majority of the campus buildings were constructed in steel, a few, for reasons of economy, were reinforced concrete structures. Of these, the apartment buildings, with their exposed, stepped-back structures infilled with brick spandrels and operating windows, derive from the Promontory Apartment building.

For some of the other campus buildings, as budgets and programs allowed, Mies continued to investigate the architectural possibilities of exposed steel construction, using the vocabulary he had developed before the war. Three buildings, the Chapel, the Commons and Crown Hall, were not required by the building code to have fireproofed structures. Together they represent a clear and concise history of steel construction unencumbered by the requirement of fire protection.

For reasons of economy only the chapel's roof structure was constructed in steel. In an earlier scheme, Mies proposed a steel frame of columns and beams enclosed with brick and glass; however, brick bearing walls in an English bond pattern replaced the columns in the final version. Still, there is great clarity in the structure as it exists. By exposing the underside of the roof structure, Mies makes clear the elements of the structure and their respective roles.

The chapel drew critical fire for its simplicity. Critics applied traditional standards and definitions to determine whether or not it constituted a religious space. Some thought it a "holy box"; others accused it of being a "power plant" masquerading as a church.[41] All the buildings for the campus, including St. Saviour Chapel and Boiler Plant, shared Mies's concern for structure, for materials and their expression, and for sensitive proportions. Critics expecting each building type to be recognizably different from all other building types overlooked the fact that when Mies established the basic spatial framework for the campus, the three-dimensional module 24 feet by 24 feet by 12 feet, he also established the architectural vocabulary for all the buildings. And within both he found great freedom to work.

St. Saviour Chapel is a simple, understated meditation space. It is logically constructed from ordinary materials ennobled by the care and sensitivity with which they have been used. By the subtlest means, a travertine altar, a stainless steel cross and a natural Shantung silk curtain, Mies embellished the space. As he described it:

"Architecture should be concerned with the epoch, not the day. The chapel will not grow old . . . it is of noble character constructed of good materials, and has beautiful proportions . . . it is done as things should be done today, taking advantage of our technological means. The men who

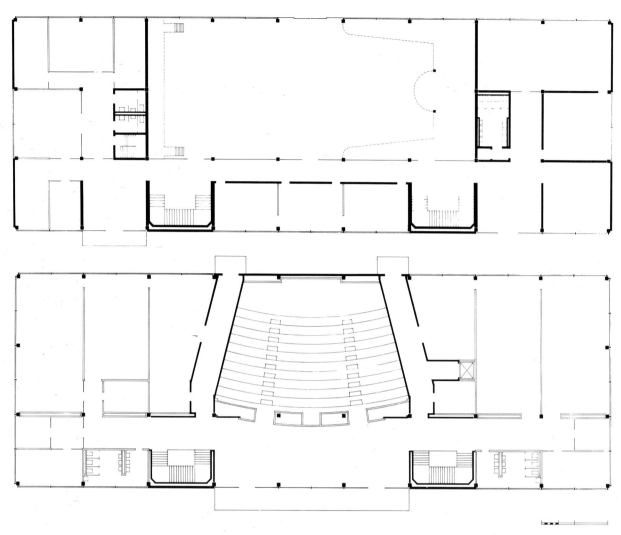

165, 166, 167. *First floor plans of Alumni Memorial Hall, Wishnick Hall, and Perlstein Hall, I.I.T., 1945–46.*

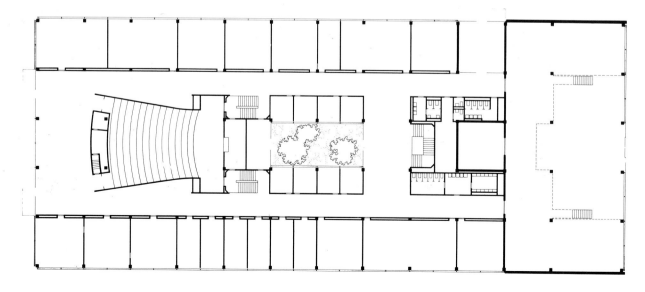

168. Classroom buildings and research facilities at I.I.T.

169. St. Savior Chapel, I.I.T., 1949–52.

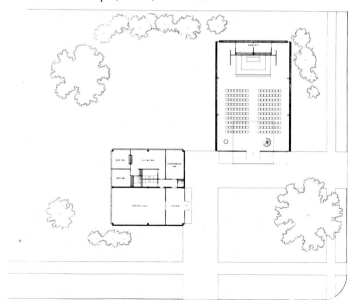

170. St. Savior Chapel. Preliminary plan.

171. St. Savior Chapel. Interior.

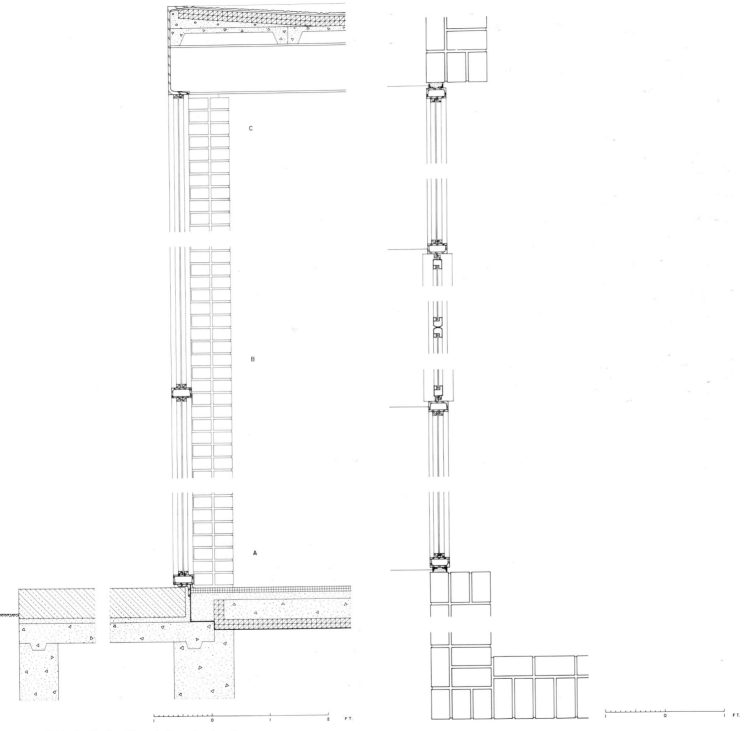

172, 173. St. Savior Chapel. Exterior details.

174. Commons building, I.I.T., 1952–53.

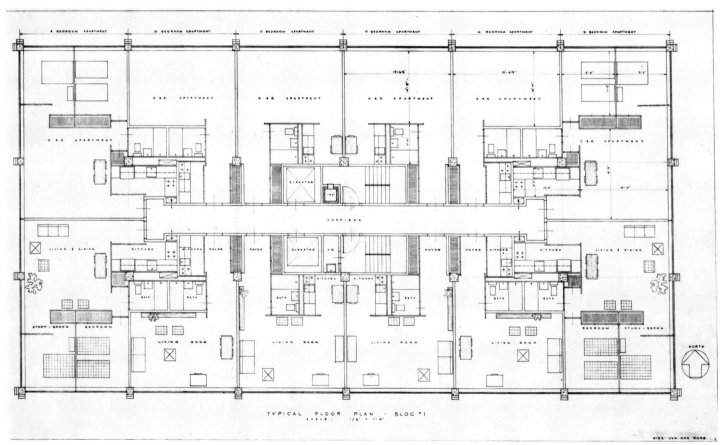

175. Carmen Hall apartment building, I.I.T., 1951–53. Typical floor plan.

146

176. Boiler plant, I.I.T., 1945–50.

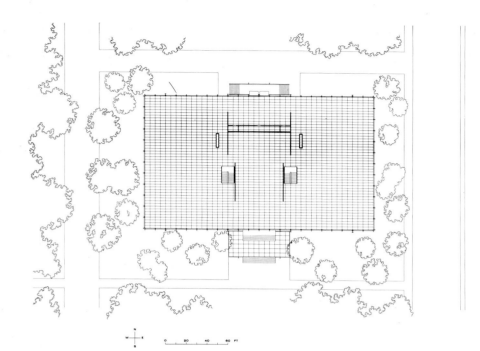

did the Gothic churches achieved the best they could with their means." [42]

The Commons has all the elements of a very complex building program. It contains medical facilities, a bookstore, post office, barber shop, dry cleaners, grocery and drug store, plus a kitchen and dining hall. Mies accommodated their different requirements within a clear, regular structure. One need know nothing of the design of structural systems to understand and appreciate the logic with which Mies has related beams, girders and columns to each other and to the whole. There is the quality of an organic solution in the manner in which equal and unequal parts have been reconciled to each other and each has been assigned its proper place.

It was in Crown Hall, housing the department of architecture and the department of city and regional planning as well as the Institute of Design (now the College of Architecture, Planning and Design), where Mies challenged the limits of structure and technology and realized the first of his large-scale "universal spaces." Four steel plate girders welded to eight H-columns form the primary structure from which the roof has been suspended. The plate girders, 6 feet 3 inches deep, span 120 feet, 60 feet on center. At either end, the roof cantilevers an additional 20 feet, so that the enclosed, column-free space is 220 feet long and 120 feet deep. Unencumbered by fireproofing and only partially subdivided by freestanding partitions 8 feet tall and 2 service cores which extended from floor to ceiling, the space is virtually uninterrupted.

One of Mies's earlier projects, the Cantor Drive-In Restaurant (1945–46), was an obvious influence in his decision to suspend Crown Hall's roof from plate girders spanning the width of the building. In the restaurant project, the roof was hung from the underside of two Pratt-type trusses spanning the long dimension of the space. As a result the interior was free of the spatial and organizational constraints interior columns make.

As Mies commented when Crown Hall neared completion, "I think this is the clearest structure we have done, the best to express our philosophy." [43] The architect Eero Saarinen (1911–61) also thought that the building made an important statement. At the dedication of Crown Hall, com-

148

179. Crown Hall under construction.

180. Crown Hall. Interior.

menting on Mies and his work, Saarinen stated:

"Great architecture is both universal and individual. . . . The universality comes because there is an architecture expressive of its time. But the individuality comes as the expression of one man's unique combination of faith and honesty and devotion and beliefs in architecture—in short, his moral integrity." [44]

Earlier in his dedicatory remarks, Saarinen was to describe Crown Hall as the "proudest" building on the IIT campus.

Not everyone, however, understood that it was a classroom building. Before an occupancy permit could be issued, a fire inspector insisted that Crown Hall be sprinklered. Unlike critics and historians who expected something more or something else, the building inspector understood, after looking at the column-free space, that Crown Hall was not like any classroom building he had seen before. Unable to classify it except by size, to his way of thinking it was "an industrial building" and required sprinklers. [45] That anonymous bureaucrat may well have paid Mies the highest compliment.

In the strictest sense, Crown Hall's two levels never warehoused anything except space. The upper level was, though, the site of several banquets and receptions, at least one jazz concert, a dance, various major exhibitions and numerous other celebrations. All the while, it remained a classroom or a series of classroom spaces. Undisturbed, different classes were conducted adjacent to each other; the sheer volume of space absorbed distracting noise. But the building's size did not prevent a student from developing a sense of place and the sense of belonging to a larger whole. The very openness of the building encouraged objectivity, an openness to teaching and learning, and free exchange among faculty and students.

The lower level housed the Institute of Design whose educational program included visual and product design, photography and printmaking, and required more conventional subdivisions of space. Within regular structural bays, 20 feet by 30 feet, of reinforced concrete columns supporting a flat slab, Mies provided classrooms, offices, workshops, a lounge and exhibition space, restrooms, and a mechanical room. Perimeter "clerestory" windows provided natural lighting to these spaces as required.

The methods Mies used to realize this space were not unique to him, only their application and execution were. The plate girder structure employed on the upper level was one frequently used for bridges, especially railway bridges. The rolled steel sections from which the structure and curtain wall were fabricated are standard mill shapes. Even the type of welded joint employed is standard so that there is the feel of mass-production about Crown Hall. It is, however, the manner in which all these elements come together, their proportion, the space they create, and the underlying clarity of expression which elevates this building above the norm and appeals to the spirit.

Crown Hall was not developed in isolation. During the six years he was at work on it, Mies was involved with several other projects of equal spatial or structural importance. The largest of these were for a new National Theater (1952–53) for Mannheim, Germany and a Convention Center (1953–54) for Chicago. Mies was one of a limited number of architects invited to submit designs for the new theater in Mannheim. In size his entry dwarfed Crown Hall. The theater's enclosed area measured 262 feet by 524 feet. Seven open trusses 26 feet 3 inches deep spanned the lesser dimension of the space. It was from these trusses that the secondary roof structure was suspended and cantilevered.

Aside from its impressive size, Mies's solution for the theater competition is worthy of attention for other reasons. Within the discipline imposed by technology, structure and materials, Mies was able to accommodate the complex program requirements which called for two acoustically isolated theaters seating 500 and 1300 persons respectively, stage equipment, and such facilities for each as dressing, practice and storage rooms. Also provided were two entrances and lobbies, within a rectangular, glass enclosed building with a clear, regular structure.

152

181. Crown Hall. Exterior.

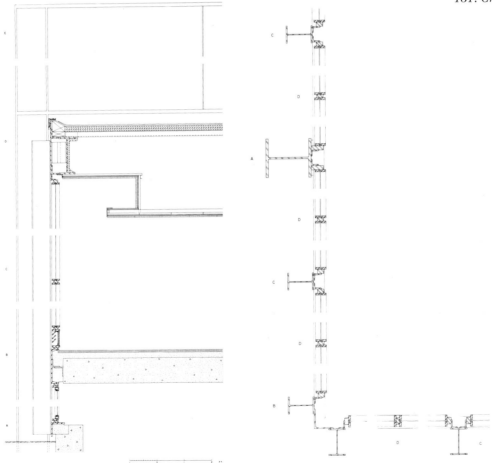

182, 183. Crown Hall. Exterior details.

153

184. *Project for a concert hall, 1942. Collage of the interior.*

185. *Cantor Drive-in Restaurant, Indianapolis, Indiana, 1945–46. Model.*

154

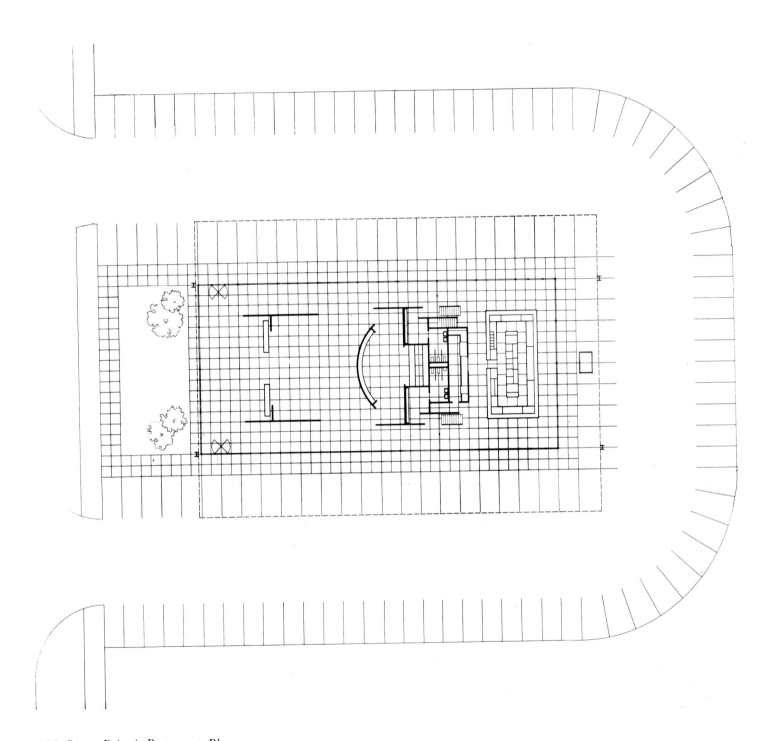

186. Cantor Drive-in Restaurant. Plan.

187. National Theater, Mannheim, Germany, 1952–53. Model.

In an earlier project for a Concert Hall (1942), Mies had located the necessary elements for the hall beneath an immense steel two-way roof structure. From this structure, as in the Mannheim project, was suspended an acoustical shell or ceiling. The actual structural prototype for the theater's open trusses first appeared in the Cantor Drive-In Restaurant project where two similar open trusses spanned the long dimension of the restaurant. The secondary roof beams were hung from these trusses cantilevering beyond them. There is a bridge-like quality to the restaurant's roof structure. Its open trusses, similar to those used in railway bridge construction, are part of the structural legacy of the Industrial Revolution. Mies was clearly interested in the spatial possibilities such structures suggested. His use of an exposed structure above the roof plane first appeared in 1942 in a museum where two open trusses spanned the auditorium space.

Through a series of projects representing different building functions, Mies explored the possibilities posed by long-span structures. The culmination of this logical investiga-

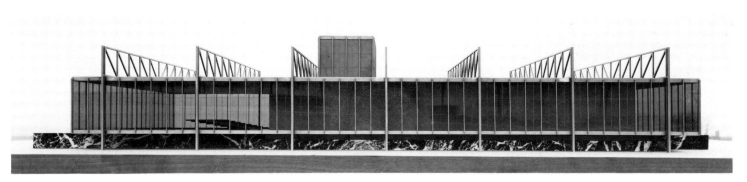

188, 189, 190. National Theater, Mannheim. Model, section, and main floor plan.

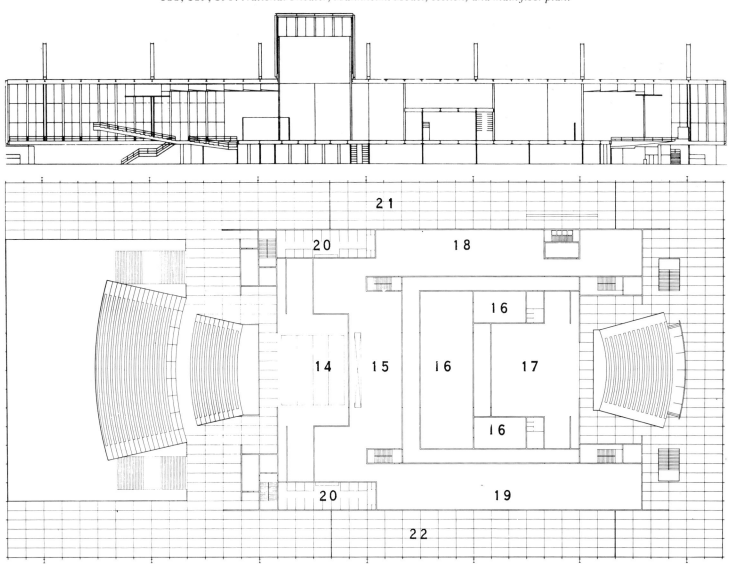

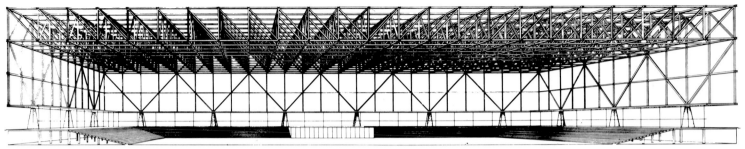

191. Convention Center, Chicago, Illinois, 1953–54. Interior perspective.

192, 193. Convention Center. Model and plan.

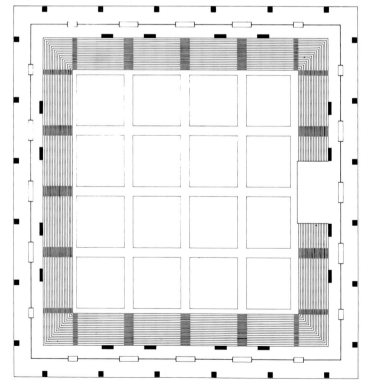

tion would have been the Chicago Convention Center. As proposed this colossal structure was 720 feet square. A series of Pratt-type trusses 30 deep 30 feet on center in both directions spanned the 500,000 square foot column-free space. The roof structure was carried on a series of trusses, 60 feet deep, which also formed the perimeter walls. The loads from these wall trusses were carried to the ground on 24 reinforced concrete supports—6 on each side.

When Mies finished the project for the Chicago Convention Center, his spatial topology was complete. The concept of universal space had been applied to a variety of architectural problems at various scales, to individual houses, apartment and office buildings, a museum, concert and exhibition halls, and to the city itself. What had once been an idea was now, for Mies, a demonstrable truth; for the remainder of his life, Mies's understanding of a universal space, like his understanding of technology, was manifested in his work.

In the design of the Convention Center, however, Mies was

158

not dependent on sheer size to convey his idea of space. It was the physical and intellectual space made possible by structure which held real fascination for him. In the more modest project referred to as the Fifty by Fifty house (1950–51), Mies defined a portion of the spatial continuum by supporting a two-way stressed roof of welded steel plates on columns centered on each side of the plan rather than located at each corner. Unlike the more conventional structure Philip Johnson employed in his residence (1949), Mies's cantilevered roof defined a portion of infinite space rather than a volume which was architecturally and spatially finite.

Space flows unimpeded in the Fifty by Fifty house. Furniture, freestanding closets, a utility core containing a kitchen, mechanical equipment for heating and air-conditioning, laundry facilities, two bathrooms, and a fireplace offer no physical obstructions. And, as in the Farnsworth house, the arrangement of fixed and moveable elements has been carefully considered and placed as a part of the architectural order. As with Frank Lloyd Wright's residential plans, all elements in the Fifty by Fifty house rotate around the hearth, which occupies the symbolic and very nearly the geometric center of the plan. The pinwheel motion in plan is further reinforced in each elevation centering floor-to-ceiling doors in the window wall to the right of the columns. By relating the paved terrace, nearly as large as the enclosed area of the house itself, asymmetrically, Mies balanced the composition and controlled the movement in plan. Solids are played against voids, horizontal planes against vertical, and fixed elements against moveable.

It was in 1955 that Mies accepted what would be his last residential commission, the Morris Greenwald house in Weston, Connecticut. Greenwald's brother, Herbert, was the developer of the apartments at 860 and 880 Lake Shore Drive in Chicago. The exterior wall of the Greenwald residence was built of portions of the curtain wall left over from the construction of 860 and 880. The plan of the house is a smaller, less successful version of Mies's Caine

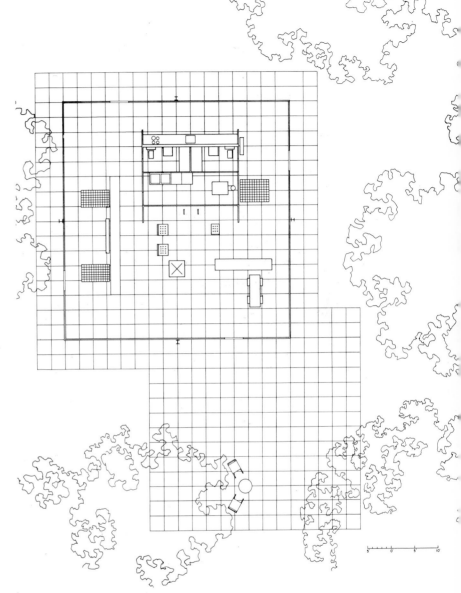

194. Fifty by Fifty house, 1950–51. Plan.

195. *Bacardi Office
Building, Santiago de
Cuba, 1957. Conte crayon
drawing of the exterior.*

160

house project (1950). In both, bedrooms and service areas flank a large, central living-dining space. However, the compact size of the Greenwald house limits the auditory privacy possible in the three bedrooms. At the client's request (and possibly because it was not as clear an architectural statement as the Farnsworth house), the house was not photographed for publication; nor was it listed among Mies's oeuvre.

Possessed by a single-mindedness of purpose, for the remainder of his life Mies pursued the goal that no contradiction should exist between architecture and structure. His solutions, as we have seen, evolved from the ideal to the specific, from structurally pure ideas (or constructs) to the necessary accommodation of and adaptation to specific functional requirements. For example, an office building project, the Cantor Commercial Center (1949–50), has a curtain wall like the steel and glass skin used on 860 and 880. The Caine house project (1950), while not elevated off the ground like the Farnsworth house, has a structure similar to it, including a cantilevered roof. The Row House project (1950–51), with an exterior structure of closely spaced steel columns reflects the skin details of 860 and 880 and anticipates the McCormick house (1951–52). The exposed steel structure of plate girders for the Cullinan Hall addition to the Houston Museum of Fine Arts (1954–58) is the same as used in Crown Hall except that the plan of the building is curved and, therefore, the plate girders are not parallel to each other. The two-way concrete roof structure resting on eight columns located along the perimeter (two on each side set in from the corners) proposed for the Bacardi Office Building, Santiago de Cuba (1957), anticipates a similar structure in steel for the New National Gallery, Berlin (1962–68). The open steel trusses proposed for one of the structural solutions at the Home Federal Savings and Loan Association Building, Des Moines (1960–63), derives directly from two earlier projects: the Cantor Drive-In Restaurant and the National Theatre, Mannheim. For Mies, architecture was "not a cocktail"[46]—something to be mixed up new everyday. It was a long, patient search.

196. Home Federal Savings and Loan building, Des Moines, Iowa, 1960–63. Preliminary model.

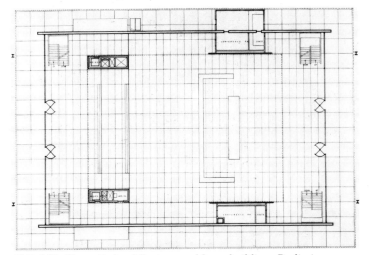

197, 198. Home Federal Savings and Loan building. Preliminary plan of the first and mezzanine floors.

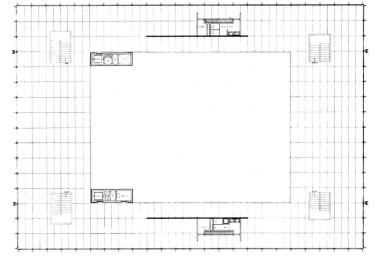

199. *Mies's sketch of the Seagram Building and plaza,*
New York City, 1954.

200. *The Seagram Building, 1954–58.*

Most often Mies's patience was rewarded. The commission for the headquarters building in New York City for Seagram Corporation (1954–58) was one such prize. Shortly after the end of World War I, Mies studied the tall office building sheathed entirely in glass. In both prismatic and curvilinear solutions (1919 and 1921), Mies's main concern was "to avoid the monotony of over-large glass surfaces." "I discovered," he continued, "by working with actual glass models that the important thing is the play of reflections and not the effect of light and shadow as in ordinary buildings."[47] Had either solution been realized, their surfaces would hardly have been monotonous or dead. They would have been the only buildings of their kind. New York City (and Chicago, for that matter) presented other problems. Whether surfaces were reflective or transparent was hardly the issue in an environment where

so many buildings were monotonous and where every one competed for attention. What was needed in a new building in such an environment was not more but less.

Kahn & Jacobs, the architects originally selected for the Seagram commission, were an old and well established New York firm. Their design was not at all different from other skyscrapers in the city with the numerous setbacks required by the zoning ordinances. And like other buildings constructed in Midtown Manhattan, their solution would have covered the entire site. Phyllis Lambert (1927–   ), daughter of Samuel Bronfman, president of Joseph E. Seagram Corporation, read about the commission while she was living in Europe. She returned home at once, and in a conversation with her father expressed her reservations about the architects' solution. The result of

162

201. The Seagram Building. The plaza.

their conversation was that *she* was charged with selecting another architect. Later she was appointed Director of Planning for the new building. In this capacity she coordinated all aspects of the work.[48]

To begin her search for an architect Lambert contacted Marie Alexander who worked at the Museum of Modern Art. Through her she met Philip Johnson, who was still serving as chairman of the museum's department of architecture. She explained that she was interested in having the proposed Seagram Building be more than just another office building in New York City and asked Johnson's assistance in the preparation of a list of architects, architectural historians and heads of architecture schools she might consult. Lambert went to see the work of every architect on Johnson's list, to meet with them, and to discuss her aspirations and expectations for the commission with them. She traveled across the country assessing what she saw. In an account of her work on the building written in 1959, she observed:

"In two and a half months of searching, it became clearer and clearer that it was Mies van der Rohe who had so understood his epoch that he made poetry of technology. In his 1950 address to the Illinois Institute of Technology Mies had said: 'Wherever technology reaches its real fulfillment, it transcends into architecture.' Through superb detailing and clarifying and articulating the structural system, Mies has given it artistic expression and created a language and vocabulary of architecture."[49]

Lambert had reached this conclusion prior to October 30, 1954, when, near the end of her search, she wrote the following assessment:

"It has been said that Frank Lloyd Wright was the greatest architect of the nineteenth century. . . . To me Johnson Wax is a complete statement of 'Manifest Destiny,' the embodiment of all the philosophy of that period in America. It has a force and vitality that is almost cyclonic. It's crazy as hell and as wonderful as it is crazy. The greatest errors of taste—not errors, just plain bad taste—turn out to be mag-

nificent. . . . His is not the statement that is needed now. America has grown up a bit and Frank Lloyd Wright has expressed what it was when its energies were unharnessed.

Le Corbusier has not built a building in this country. (The UN was unfortunately only an emasculation of his plan.) Would he be a great influence here? I am afraid not. . . . One is fascinated by his spaces, his sculptural forms, but are not people likely to be blinded by these and skip over the surface only? Mies forces you in. You have to go deeper. You might think this austere strength, this ugly beauty, is terribly severe. It is, and yet all the more beauty in it.

The younger men, the second generation (of the modern movement), are talking in terms of Mies or denying him. They talk of new forms—articulating the skin of facades to get a play of light and shadow. But Mies has said, 'Form is not the aim of our work, only the result.' In his Farnsworth house in 1951 and the Twin Towers at 860 Lake Shore Drive in Chicago in 1952, he has articulated the skin, at the same time creating a play of depth and shadow by the use of the basic structural steel member, the I beam. This ingenious and deceptively simple solution is comparable to the use of the Greek orders and the Flying Buttress. It is not a capricious solution; it is the essence of the problem of modern architecture that Mies stated in 1922: 'We should develop the new forms from the very nature of the new problems.'"[50]

Mies was awarded the commission. Because he was not a registered architect in New York State, he asked Philip Johnson, who was, to associate with him on the commission. They rented office space and began work. Johnson's role was to coordinate work between Mies's Chicago office and the New York office. When the Seagram Corporation decided to include the Four Seasons restaurant in the building, Mies asked Johnson to design it.

For several years previously, Seagram Corporation had been acquiring land for the new building. The site selected was essentially a peninsula bounded on three sides by streets. Park Avenue forms the western edge and Fifty-second and Fifty-third Streets are the boundaries to the

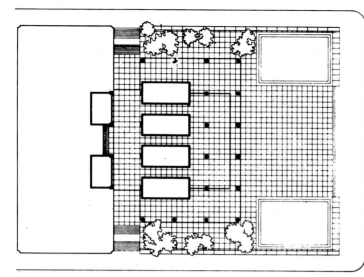

202, 203, 204. *The Seagram Building. Plaza level and typical intermediate and tower floor plans.*

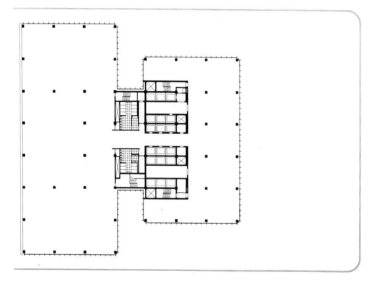

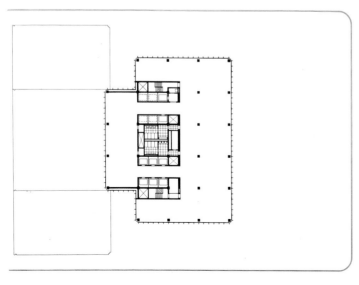

south and north respectively. A line of existing buildings to the east forms the fourth side of a rectangle 200 by 300 feet. Between Park Avenue and the existing buildings to the east, there is a drop in elevation of nearly eight feet. The client's only program requirements were that the new headquarters provide 500,000 square feet of useable rental space and that the building be the "crowning glory of everyone's work"[51]—the client's, the general contractor's and Mies's.

Existing zoning regulations and setback requirements limited how the site could be developed. Attempting to avoid the usual setbacks, Mies explored three possibilities for a freestanding tower: a square tower; a rectangular tower proportioned 7:3 with the shorter side parallel to Park Avenue (a solution similar to Skidmore, Owings, & Merrill's Lever House (1952) just north and diagonally opposite the site); and a smaller rectangular tower proportioned 5:3 with the longer side parallel to Park Avenue set back ninety feet from the street.[52] As Lambert stated in a letter dated December 1, 1954, Mies appeared to be leaning in favor of the third possibility:

"This solution for the building has promise for terrific things—set back you hardly see it from the street coming up or down the Avenue but *now what an impression—when you arrive there—almost Baroque, you don't know what is there and then you come upon IT—with a magnificent plaza and the building not zooming up in front of your nose so that you can't see it, only be oppressed by it and have to cross the street to really look at it,* but a magnificent *entrance to a* magnificent *building all in front of you—How excited I get just thinking of it—Oh how right the decision of Mies is—I become more convinced everyday . . ."*[53]

By preserving nearly half of the site as open space, the building could be a simple, freestanding tower uninterrupted by setbacks. The resulting plaza was a magnanimous, costly and wonderfully humane gesture. While the plaza provided the Seagram Building with a handsome setting, Mies intended that this open space be more than an expensive, unused front yard. It is one of New York

City's most successful open spaces: paving of pink granite, two pools with fountains, marble benches, and gingko trees planted in beds of ivy enlivened the open space and beckon passersby for a short, restful pause or lunch *alfresco*.

The plaza appears more spacious because Mies incorporated streets and sidewalks beyond the property into the overall composition. Neither the benches, which parallel Fifty-second and Fifty-third Streets, nor the low steps along Park Avenue are visually strong enough (or tall enough) to contain the plaza's space. Only the tightly packed buildings on the other side of the streets do that. There is, also, the formal relationship Mies established between the Seagram Building and its neighbor, the Racquet and Tennis Club (1916–19) by McKim, Mead & White, directly across Park Avenue. Both structures are symmetrical, with their respective entrances directly opposite each other, establishing a connection which bridges the street. As a result, Park Avenue becomes an amenity integral with the Seagram site and is no longer merely a landscaped, isolated zone for the automobile.

On the site, the granite paving of the plaza extends into and through the glass enclosed lobby, which is twenty-four feet high. No rental space encroaches upon this flow of space. In the lobby there are only the necessary elevator and mechnical cores, and these Mies has sheathed with Roman travertine. Above, supported on bronze clad columns, rise thirty-nine floors of corporate and rental office space, enclosed with a skin of glass tinted topaz-gray, set in bronze frames with bronze mullions and spandrels. Directly behind the tower, existing buildings adjacent to the site are screened from the plaza's view by a five-story structure containing additional corporate and rental space, which is also enclosed with the same curtain wall of glass and bronze. Further, the slope of the site allows deliveries and the entrance to the parking garage to be accommodated below the plaza level.

The rich materials and unprecedented open space endowed the Seagram Building with a monumentality without equal in either the civic or religious architecture of our time. It set a new standard for corporate and rental offices, and today is still a monument to the American corporation and both the symbol and the metaphor of its age. But not everyone saw it as such: one critic, historian Lewis Mumford, likened it to a "pyramid—a building that exhausts every resource of art and engineering to create an imposing visible effect out of all proportion to its human significance."[54]

As critical attitudes were articulated, positions clarified and assessments made (and assessments made of assessments), Mies remained aloof and detached. He had made a fine building which, apart from pleasing both the client and himself, also gratified the people who sat on the benches, were refreshed by the fountains and shaded by the trees, who, in all probability, sensed that this building

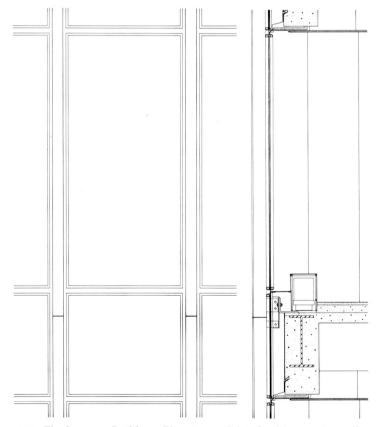

205. The Seagram Building. Elevation and details of the curtain wall.

was a monument to an idea first and to a corporation second. It made a gesture to the quality of urban life in an age not given to such gestures. As a cab driver said, looking first at Lever House across the street and then at the Seagram Building: "The copy doesn't usually get built before the original, does it?"[55]

In 1984 the American Institute of Architects bestowed its 25-Year Award on the Seagram Building formally recognizing Mies's contributions to architecture and urban design. In their remarks, the jury commented that "25 years after its completion, it fully retains its enduring vitality and quiet beauty, and still holds a special place in the hearts and imaginations of all who see it, work in it, and admire its brilliant solution to the still-vexing problems of urban design."[56] For Mies, though, the Seagram Building was not essentially different from his other work. As he explained it:

"My concept and approach on the Seagram Building was no different from that of any other building that I might build. My idea, or better 'direction,' in which I go is toward a clear structure and construction—this applies not to any one problem but to all architectural problems which I approach. I am, in fact, completely opposed to the idea that a specific building should have an individual character. Rather, a universal character which has been determined by the total problem which architecture must strive to solve.

On the Seagram Building, since it was to be built in New York and since it was to be the first major office building which I was to build, I asked for two types of advice for the development of the plans. One, the best real estate advice as to the types of desirable rentable space and, two, professional advice regarding the New York City Building Code. With my direction established and, with these advisers, it was then only a matter of hard work."[57]

Prior to the Seagram Building's completion, most, if not all, rental office space in New York City was constructed at the lowest possible cost. The formula for calculating real estate taxes was predicated on this fact. However, as the Seagram Building cost $36 million to build, with an addi-

tional $5 million spent for land acquisition, using the existing tax formula to calculate its annual tax bill would have resulted in a loss of tax revenue for the city of a potential extra $300,000 annually. The "taxable value" formula, argued attorneys for the city of New York, overlooked the Seagram Building's "prestige value." The case was taken to court where, after extensive litigation, it was finally decided by New York State's highest court, the Court of Appeals. The court ruled in favor of New York City upholding the position that certain "prestige" office buildings should be taxed on their "real replacement value." Critics, including Ada Louise Huxtable, argued before the final decision that special tax categories would spell "architectural annihilation" for New York City.[58]

The great success of the Seagram Building brought Mies wider recognition and important new commissions, which were, generally, on the scale of the Seagram Building. In 1958 the Bronfmans retained him to make feasibility studies for a site (actually two sites separated by a street) along Chicago's North Michigan Avenue which they were considering for development. What Mies proposed was a group of rental structures rather than a single tower. The studies were carried out and a model built, but the project went no further.

Concurrent with the Seagram commission was Mies's development of a master plan for the expansion of the Houston Museum of Fine Arts. Increasing the gallery space was only one aspect of a larger and more ambitious plan for increasing both the stature and scope of the collection. For the first phase to expand the gallery space, Mies proposed Cullinan Hall (1954–58). The structure of this large exhibition space is similar to Crown Hall's where the roof is suspended from four steel-plate girders overhead. However, Crown Hall is a more general solution to the problem of finding an appropriate architectural solution for large, undifferentiated space because it is a freestanding building. The plan for Cullinan Hall is a result of the influence the adjacent museum exerted on Mies; the exhibition space fills a trapezoidal space between the unsymmetrical wings

206, 207. *Cullinan Hall, Museum of Fine Arts, Houston, Texas, 1954–58.*

169

of the museum. The plan displays Mies's ability to create order from disorder as well as his determination to pursue clarity of structure and the universality of space as ideas central to all of his work.

Since his arrival in the United States, Mies had become one of the most highly regarded architects and educators in the twentieth century. Chicago, and to an increasing extent the rest of the nation, provided him with the benign environment Germany under Hitler had denied him. No longer was his reputation dependent upon a few projects and a few completed buildings. After two decades in Chicago, Mies had realized a solid and important body of completed works as well as a number of important projects. His school flourished, attracting undergraduate and graduate students from all over the world. If the school was not widely imitated, other students as well as practicing architects paid Chicago, the IIT campus, and especially Crown Hall seemingly obligatory visits as part of their education. At Crown Hall they saw Mies's work as well as the work of the school. It remained the most accessible of Mies's buildings, the clearest expression of his ideas about architecture and education.

After twenty years as director of the department of architecture, in declining health, and with his practice demanding more of his attention, Mies resigned his faculty appointment. He fully expected to stay on as campus architect. But this was not to be. In spite of letters and telegrams (including one from Le Corbusier) urging IIT's Board of Trustees to retain Mies as campus architect, the board appointed the Chicago-based firm of Skidmore, Owings & Merrill to be architects for the campus. As Mies recalled shortly after his resignation:

". . . they [the board of trustees] decided that it was better to work with other people and have some local man in the field. They then felt they had made a mistake by doing that and they asked me to make one of the other buildings. I said: 'No. The campus was planned as a unit and, if it cannot be a unit, I have to be satisfied with a torso.'"[59]

Thus, Mies's and IIT's long and mutually beneficial relationship ended in a cloud of misunderstanding with rancor on both sides as a residue.

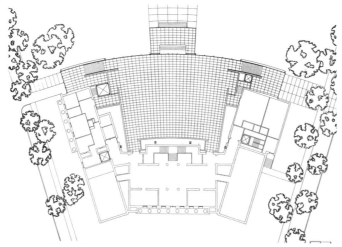

208. Cullinan Hall. First floor plan.

1 John Entenza, "The Presentation of the Gold Medal, Chicago Chapter, American Institute of Architects" (Graham Foundation for Advanced Studies in the Fine Arts: 1966), 3–4.

2 In 1937, a year before Mies's arrival, László Moholy-Nagy moved to Chicago and founded a school, The New Bauhaus. Though limited in scope, in idea The New Bauhaus grew directly out of Moholy-Nagy's experiences as a member of the Bauhaus faculty in Weimar and Dessau. In 1939 the name of the school was changed to the Institute of Design. The Institute existed as a separate entity until 1949 when it merged with IIT and became a department within the university.

3 Katherine Kuh, "Mies van der Rohe, Modern Classicist," Saturday Review 48 (January 23, 1956): 61.

4 Peter Carter, "Mies van der Rohe, an appreciation on the Occasion, This Month, of his 75th Birthday," Architectural Design 31 (March 1961): 115.

5 Ludwig Hilberseimer, "Amerikanische Architektur," G (Berlin), no. 4 (March 1926): 4.

6 Henry T. Heald, "Mies van der Rohe at I.I.T.," Four Great Makers of Modern Architecture (New York: Columbia University Press, 1963), 106.

7 Personal communication with George Danforth.

8 "Armour's Architect," Time 32 (September 12, 1938): 50.

9 Ludwig Mies van der Rohe, [Address to the 37th Association of Collegiate Schools of Architecture Annual Convention,] Journal of Architectural Education 7 (Summer 1951): 13–15.

10 Philip Johnson, Mies van der Rohe (New York: Museum of Modern Art, 1953), 196–200.

11 Notes from Alfred Caldwell's second year construction class at IIT.

12 Heald, "Mies van der Rohe at I.I.T.," 107.

13 Kuh, "Mies van der Rohe, Modern Classicist," 61.

14 Carter, "Mies van der Rohe, an appreciation," 105.

15 Ibid.

16 Ibid.

17 "Metals and Minerals Research Building, Illinois Institute of Technology," Architectural Forum 79 (November 1943): 88.

18 Peter Carter, Mies van der Rohe at Work (New York: Praeger, 1973), 10.

19 Johnson, Mies van der Rohe, 138.

20 "Drawings for the Library and Administration Building, Illinois Institute," Architects' Journal 103 (January 3, 1946): 11.

21 Peter Blake, "Ludwig Mies van der Rohe," Architectural Forum 87 (November 1947): 132.

22 Charles Eames, "Museum of Modern Art Exhibit," Arts and Architecture 64 (December 1947): 24–27.

23 "Presentation of the Royal Gold Medal for 1959 to Ludwig Mies van der Rohe," Journal of the Royal Institute of British Architects 66 (July 1959): 308.

24 Personal correspondence with Philip Johnson.

25 "Glass House Stones; Farnsworth House," Newsweek 41 (June 8, 1953): 90.

26 Elizabeth Gordon, "The Threat to the Next America," House Beautiful 95 (April, 1953): 250.

27 Ibid., 129.

28 "Mies' Farnsworth House Wins 25 Yr. Award," American Institute of Architects Journal 70 (March 1981): 9.

29 Ibid., 12.

30 James Marston Fitch, "Mies van der Rohe and the Platonic Virtues," Four Great Makers of Modern Architecture (New York: Columbia University Press, 1963), 163.

31 "House at New Canaan, Connecticut," Architectural Review 108 (September 1950): 154.

32 Institute of Architecture and Urban Studies, Philip Johnson: Processes [Catalogue 9] (New York: Institute for Architecture and Urban Studies, 1978), 51.

33 These figures are 1952 and 1950 costs, respectively.

34 "Apartments . . . ," Architectural Forum 92 (January 1950): 70.

35 "Mies van der Rohe's New Buildings," Architectural Forum (November 1952): 99.

36 Herbert Jacobs, Frank Lloyd Wright: America's Greatest Architect (New York: Harcourt, Brace & World, Inc., 1965), 183.

37 Personal communication with Bernard Goodman, one of Mies's students at IIT.

38 So as not to compete with or detract from 860 and 880, the curtain wall of the Esplanade Apartments has a matt black rather than a natural aluminum finish.

39 Ludwig Mies van der Rohe, "Bürohaus," G (Berlin), no. 1 (June 1923): 3.

40 Carter, Mies van der Rohe at Work, 177.

41 Philip Johnson, "Annual Discourse 1979," Royal Institute of British Architects Journal 86 (July 1979): 330.

42 "Mies van der Rohe: A Chapel," Arts and Architecture 70 (January 1953): 19.

43 Carter, "Mies van der Rohe, an appreciation," 110.

44 "IIT Dedicates Crown Hall, New Design Building by Mies," Architectural Forum 104 (June 1956): 21.

45 "An Architecture Building for I.I.T.," Architectural Record 120 (August 1956): 136.

46 "Mies Speaks.," Architectural Review, 452.

47 Ludwig Mies van der Rohe, "Hochhaus Project für Bahnhof Friedrichstrasse in Berlin," Frülicht 1 (1922): 122.

48 Phyllis Lambert, "How a Building Gets Built," Vassar Alumnae Magazine (February 1959): 16.

49 Ibid., 14.

50 Ibid., 14, 16.

51 Ibid., 16.

52 Ibid., 17.

53 Ibid., 17–18.

54 Lewis Mumford, "Skyline: The Lesson of the Master," New Yorker 34 (September 13, 1958): 148.

55 From a classroom discussion with Myron Goldsmith, Adjunct Professor of Architecture at IIT.

56 "The Seagram Building Wins AIA's 25-Year Award," American Institute of Architects Journal 74 (April 1984): 25.

57 Carter, "Mies van der Rohe, an appreciation," 115.

58 Ada Louise Huxtable, "Legislating Against Quality," The New York Times Sec. 2 (May 26, 1963): 11.

59 H. T. Cadbury-Brown, Ludwig Mies van der Rohe: "An Address of Appreciation," Architecture Association Journal 75 (July 1959): 35.

Page 172

209. New National Gallery, Berlin, Germany, 1962–68.

CHAPTER V: 1959-1969

Mies continues to be our consience, but who listens to his conscience these days.[1]
—Harry Weese, 1966

In 1960 Mies was awarded the American Institute of Architects (AIA) Gold Medal for distinguished service to the profession. In terms of professional recognition, Mies had reached the apex of his career. A year earlier the Royal Institute of British Architects (RIBA) awarded Mies its highest award, also a Gold Medal. His acceptance speech to the RIBA was characteristically brief, but noteworthy for the description of his education as an architect. As he recalled for the audience assembled in London:

"I once asked somebody to tell me what architecture was and he replied, 'Do not ask silly questions.' But I do ask them. That was all we could get. We had to start. We learned from a great man and his talents, but we did not get a clear direction. I learned more from old buildings than from this man—the old buildings with their fine, simple purpose, their fine, simple construction, their marvelous draughts-manship and wonderful proportion and unsophisticatedness. That is where I learned. These old buildings have been a continuous inspiration to me even today.

We had to find our way and we had to ask hundreds of questions . . ."[2]

As one might have expected, Mies's acceptance speech to the AIA was somewhat longer, the debt to his adopted homeland being greater. Like some euclidean geometrician affirming his definitions, postulates and axioms, Mies took the opportunity of the acceptance speech to restate the principles underlying his work and to thank the institute for its recognition.

"Teaching and working have convinced me, above all, of the need for clarity in thought and action.

Without clarity, there can be no understanding.

And without understanding, there can be no direction—only confusion.

Sometimes it is even a confusion of great men, like the time around 1900, when Wright, Berlage, Behrens, Olbrich, Loos and Van de Velde were all at work, each taking a different direction.

I have been asked many times by students, architects and interested laymen: 'Where do we go from here?'

Certainly it is not necessary nor possible to invent a new kind of architecture every Monday morning.

We are not at the end, but at the beginning of an epoch; an epoch which will be guided by a new spirit, which will be driven by new forces, new technological, sociological and economic forces, and which will have new tools and new materials. For this reason we will have a new architecture.

But the future comes not by itself. Only if we do our work in the right way will it make a good foundation for the future. In all these years I have learned more and more that

173

architecture is not a play with forms. I have come to under-stand the close relationship between architecture and civili-zation. I have learned that architecture must stem from the sustaining and driving forces of civilization and that it can be, at its best, an expression of the innermost structure of its time.

The structure of civilization is not simple, being in part the past, in part the present and in part the future. It is difficult to define and to understand. Nothing of the past can be changed by its very nature. The present has to be accepted and should be mastered. But the future is open—open for creative thought and action.

This is the structure from which architecture emerges. It follows, then, that architecture should be related only to the most significant forces in the civilization. Only a relation-ship which touches the essence of the time can be real. This relation I like to call a truth relation. Truth in the sense of Thomas Aquinas: As the Adequatio intellectus et rei. *Or, as a modern philosopher expresses it, in the language of today:* Truth is the significance of facts.

Only such a relation is able to embrace the complex nature of civilization. Only so, will architecture be involved in the evolution of civilization. And only so, will it express the slow unfolding of its form.

This has been, and will be, the task of architecture. A difficult task, to be sure. But Spinoza has taught us that great things are never easy. They are as difficult as they are rare." [3]

With a patience which by now had become legendary, Mies pursued his vision of architecture heedless of critics and fashion. He achieved nearly everything in the profes-sional sense that an architect could hope to achieve in a lifetime. As a result of his strength of personality and the integrity of his work, he became the architectural con-science of his time. His work became the standard against which the work of other architects was measured. Many architects found Mies's standards too exacting. Others

chafed at working in his shadow. Aware of this attitude but, at the same time, perplexed by it, Mies observed: "I get up. I sit on the bed. I think 'What the hell went wrong? We showed them what to do.'" [4] It was not really a question of where Mies had gone wrong. Rather, it was easier for architects with lesser talents to blame Mies for being so good than it was for them to accept the limitations of their own abilities. Many indulged themselves by choosing to believe that growing up and working in Mies's shadow (or Wright's or Gropius's or Le Corbusier's) had inhibited their professional development.

As Mies aged, critical reaction to his work became more negative. This "reaction" to his work prompted him to make the following observations shortly before his death:

"I have tried to make architecture for a technological so-ciety. . . . I have wanted to keep everything reasonable and clear—to have an architecture that anybody can do. . . . Some people say that what I do is 'cold.' That is ridiculous. You can say that a glass of milk is warm or cold. But not architecture. You can be bored with architecture, however. I am bored by this stuff I see around me. It has no logic or reason." [5]

During the 1960s Mies's office was occupied with more and larger commissions. Only one building type, the large hall with a clear span, eluded him. Of his completed works, Crown Hall and Cullinan Hall might be considered large; neither, however, approached the massive size of the 720-foot square Chicago Convention Center which remained unbuilt. However, in 1962, at age of 76, Mies was awarded the commission for the New National Gallery, Berlin (1962–68). The gallery was Mies's first and only commis-sion from the West German government. With it the op-portunity to realize a large, truly universal space was finally within his grasp. Given his advancing age, there was the very real probability that this commission might be his last major work.

The program called for a large space for the temporary exhibition of paintings and sculpture, as well as smaller

210. New National Gallery. Interior view of the upper level gallery.

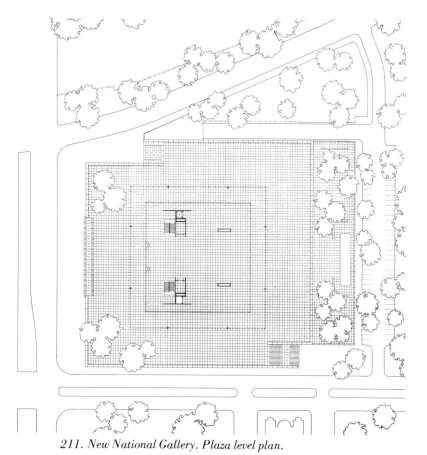

211. New National Gallery. Plaza level plan.

galleries for the museum's permanent collection. In addition there were to be offices, storage and work spaces, and a sculpture garden. Taking advantage of the sloped site, Mies located the smaller galleries, service functions and the sculpture garden on the building's lower level. As a result, the garden is on grade (for ease of moving large sculptures in and out) and open to the sky. Certain of the smaller exhibition spaces also receive natural light.

The lower level forms a base or platform for the major exhibition hall. The effect of this platform is to isolate the hall from the immediate context of the site. While the other buildings in West Berlin's Kemperplatz culture center compete with each other for attention, the New National Gallery stands apart, special in its isolation . . . and timelessness. Of all Mies's buildings, it is his most classical in feeling. It is a temple to art on a man-made acropolis.

The museum is, however, a product of its own time. Its impressive two-way roof structure of welded steel plates is statically indeterminate to the thirty-sixth degree and only capable of solution through the use of a computer.[6] As in Mies's other buildings, the New National Gallery's qualities as a space are the product of the technology and materials of the twentieth century working in conjunction with his idea of an architecturally defined spactial continuum.

Structurally and spatially the museum bears an obvious resemblance to one of Mies's earlier projects, the Bacardi Office Building (1957), Santiago de Cuba. Although the museum's structure is larger, and of steel versus reinforced concrete for the Bacardi building, both have square plans. Each employs a two-way roof structure supported along the perimeter on eight columns (two on each side set in from the corners). Each defines large open spaces on an elevated platform. Further, Mies used broad flights of steps reminiscent of Schinkel's work to connect their respective platforms with the ground.

It is in their interior arrangement of space that the two buildings most clearly differ from each other. With its single mechanical core, stairway and unequal lengths of low storage units, the spatial arrangement of the Bacardi

176

Building is asymmetrical, a decided contrast to the bilateral symmetry of the New National Gallery's first-floor plan. Both demonstrate the freedom with which Mies approached the organization of space and, in return, the freedom of organization such universal spaces afforded him.

In the Bacardi Building a series of walls beyond the perimeter of the roof structure define exterior spaces. Along one of these walls and stretching the entire length of the paved podium was to have been a reflecting pool animated by a double row of small fountains. There is about every aspect of this project, like the museum, the quality of timelessness and repose which Mies achieved by endowing the necessary structural and program requirements with a ceremonial grandeur and monumentality commonly associated with religious rather than secular architecture.

As apparent in the quality of the Seagram Building, Mies raised the rental office building to the realm of art. The same is true of the other commissions for office buildings which were awarded to him following completion of Seagram. In addition to office buildings, there were commissions for numerous apartment buildings, a project for a museum, a large addition to a museum, an automobile service station, three academic buildings, a library, and projects for a broadcasting studio, and a kindergarten-through-fourth-grade school. Such a listing is impressive in its diversity.

The office complex which served as the prototype for other large developments was the Federal Center Complex (1959–73) in Chicago, which Mies designed as a joint venture with three other Chicago architecture firms: Schmidt,

212. New National Gallery and adjacent buildings in the Kemperplatz.

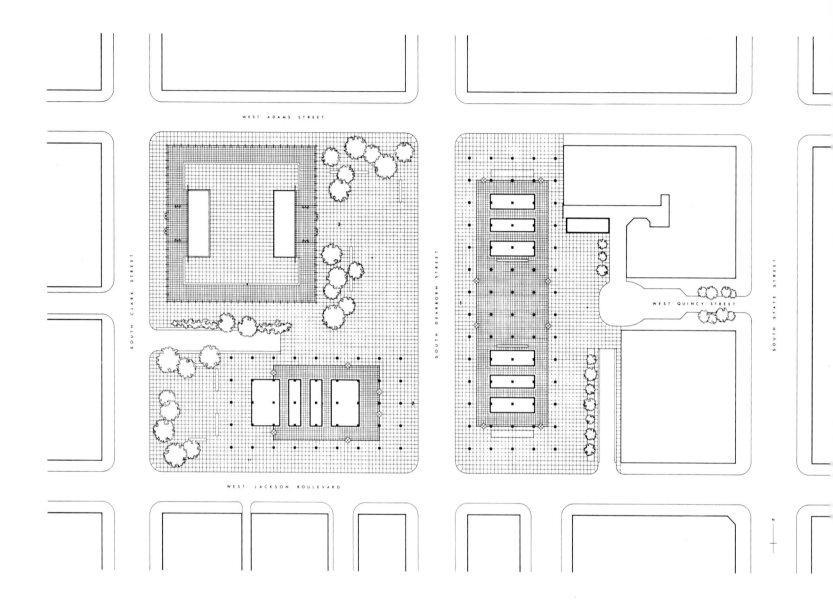

213. Federal Center complex. Chicago, Illinois, 1959–73. Plaza level plan.

178

Garden & Erickson; C. F. Murphy Associates; and A. Epstein & Sons, Inc. The Federal Center Complex consists of three freestanding structures—a thirty-story courthouse and office building, a forty-two-story office building, and a one-story post office—that have been arranged on a 4½-acre site in such a way as to create a series of interrelated open spaces, the largest of which is similar in size to the Seagram Building plaza. Mies used light gray granite to pave the open spaces and the lobbies of the three buildings. As a result, there is a continuity between interior and exterior spaces, an increase in the apparent size of the individual spaces and a sense of expansiveness throughout the complex. The Federal Center gave Mies his first opportunity to create a major urban space with freestanding buildings in the congested heart of the business district of a major city. Because the site was less densely developed than allowed by the building code, the large open spaces make a humane civic gesture.

As much for his contributions to American architecture as for his work on the Chicago Federal Center, President John F. Kennedy selected Mies for the Presidential Medal of Freedom in 1963. This was an especially fitting tribute from a man who valued achievement and excellence to one whose work had come to symbolize the best of post-war architecture in the United States. Mies was deeply moved by this tribute. It indicated appreciation of his work by an audience not confined to his fellow professionals.

214. President John F. Kennedy nominated Mies for the Medal of Freedom, and President Lyndon B. Johnson made the actual presentation of the award on December 6, 1963, two weeks after Kennedy's assassination.

215. *Frederich Krupp Administration Building, Essen, Germany, 1959–63. Model.*

Three projects were concurrent with the early work on the Federal Center: the Rockville Center Development (1959), Rockville, Maryland; the Friedrich Krupp Administration Building, Essen, Germany (1959–63); and the Schaefer Museum, Schweinfurt, Germany (1960–61).

Mies endowed the Krupp Building with a sense of repose and a spaciousness appropriate to a corporate client. These are the same qualities found in the Seagram Building and the Federal Center. The difference is that the Krupp Building was to have been a low building not a highrise. For

Krupp, Mies proposed elevating the two floors of offices above a paved platform or base which contained parking, mechanical services, and facilities for a kitchen and restaurant. The offices surround two open, landscaped courts which flank the building's entrance. The quality of understated monumentality in the Krupp Building recalls Mies's earlier project for the Silk Industry Administration Building, Krefeld (1933).

It is both instructive and satisfying to see many of Mies's fertile ideas reborn in later work. Such was the case in his

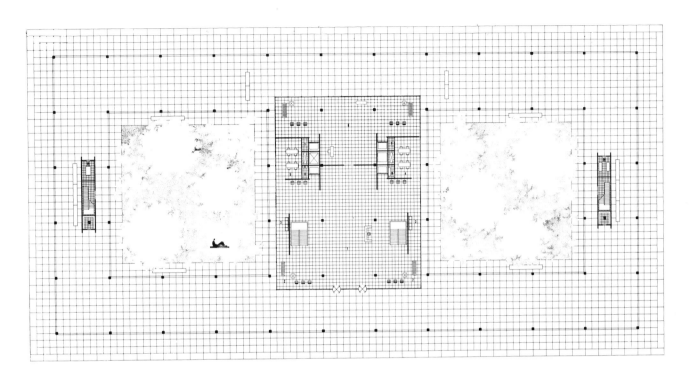

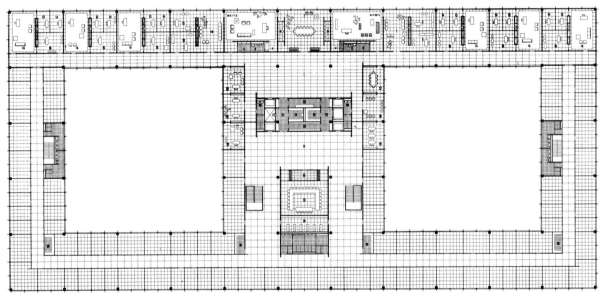

216, 217. *Frederich Krupp Administration Building. Plaza level and typical office floor plan.*

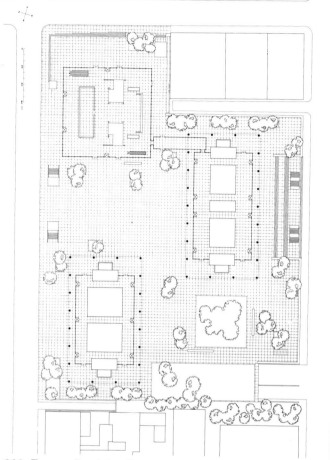

218. Toronto-Dominion Center, Toronto, Canada, 1963–69. Plaza
level plan.

219. Toronto-Dominion Center.

preliminary solution for the Home Federal Savings and
Loan Association Building, Des Moines (1960–63). Here
Mies proposed using a slightly different version of the
structure developed for the Cantor Drive-In Restaurant
(1945–46). As in the restaurant, the roof of the Home
Federal Building was to have been suspended and cantilevered from the underside of two exposed, open steel
trusses. These trusses spanned the long dimension of the
building and were supported on four columns—two at
either end. Unlike the restaurant, which was a single-story
space, the main banking hall of Home Federal was to have
been surrounded by a balcony containing open office space,
and suspended from tension rods attached to the trusses
overhead. This solution was structurally and spatially more
interesting than the one finally accepted by the board of
directors, who, after the initial scheme was presented to
them, decided to expand the building's program to include
rental office space. The change in program necessitated a
change in structure.

The final solution to Home Federal owes much to Mies's
concurrent work for Krupp. Both have square structural
bays. Both have two floors of offices elevated above an
entrance space, which in the Home Federal Building is
also the main banking hall. And both have skin details
similar to those Mies used in the 860 and 880 Lake Shore
Drive Apartments (1945–51), where the size and expression of the columns interrupted the rhythm of the windows
but not the regularity of the window mullions themselves.
To Mies's way of thinking, when there was reason for
change, he changed. When he could refine an earlier
solution, he did so.

There were other commissions which came to Mies as the
result of his work for Seagram. These commissions were
for sites in Canada (Seagram's corporate home) and in-
cluded: Mountain Place project, Montreal (1961); Toronto-
Dominion Center, Toronto (1963–69); Westmount Square,
Montreal (1965–68); three apartment buildings for the
Nun's Island Development, Montreal (1967–69); an Esso
Service Station (1967–68) also for Nun's Island; and the
Dominion Square project, Montreal (1968–69). Of these,

TORONTO DOMINION BANK

220. Toronto-Dominion Center. Underground shopping mall.

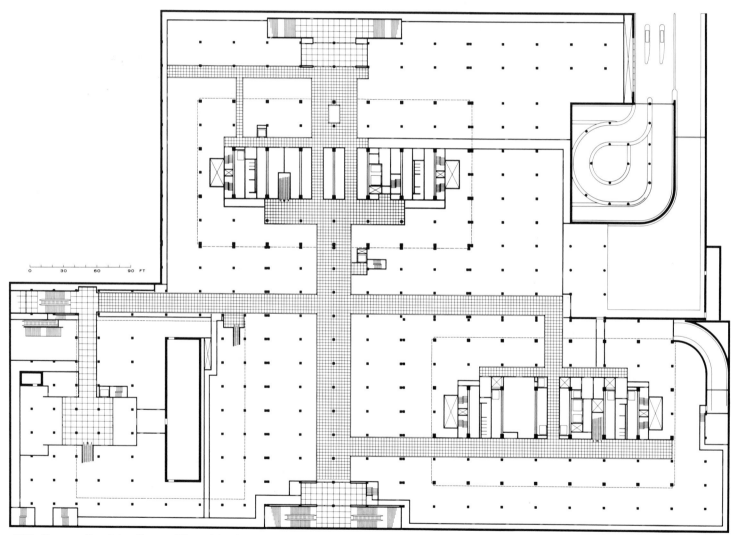

221. Toronto-Dominion Center. Plan of the shopping concourse.

184

Toronto-Dominion Center and Westmount Square are the most interesting because of their mixed land use. In each a concourse below grade containing a variety of shops and restaurants and a cinema is linked with office buildings above and, in the case of Westmount Square, apartment buildings, arranged on a paved, landscaped plaza.

While a few architects prior to Mies had designed mixed-use developments (Rockefeller Center, 1931–34, in New York City is an obvious example), few, if any, had achieved the physical and aesthetic unity of these two Canadian developments. Like the Federal Center in Chicago, in the Toronto-Dominion Center and Westmount Square there was a concern for the pedestrian and a refreshingly humane sense of openness. In these automobile-free precincts Mies created, individuals and groups can enjoy their leisure time in sunlit, landscaped spaces. By raising the place of work to the realm of art, Mies ennobled work itself.

In contrast to the planning and design control Mies exercised in these large developments, his work in the renewal of downtown Baltimore was limited to one office building: One Charles Center (1960–63). Because of economic considerations, reinforced concrete was substituted for steel as the structural material and, as it turned out, One Charles Center became the prototype for Mies's later office buildings in concrete, just as the 900 and 910 Lake Shore Drive Apartments (1953–56) were the prototypes for all his later, air-conditioned apartment buildings with reinforced concrete structures. Other office buildings in reinforced concrete included the Westmount Square in Montreal, and One Illinois Center, Chicago (1967–70). Apartment buildings at Westmount Square also had structures of reinforced concrete as did those at Nun's Island. The prototype for the Nun's Island apartment buildings was Highfield House, Baltimore (1963–65).

At the time of his eightieth birthday, Mies was involved in still more office buildings. Five of these, however, remained unbuilt: the Blue Cross Building, Chicago (1966–69); the foreign branch headquarters for Lloyds Bank, London (1967); the Commerzbank AG, Frankfurt/Main

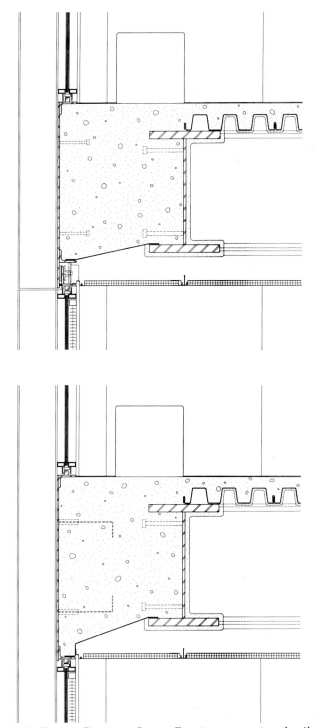

222. *Toronto-Dominion Center. Exterior construction details.*

185

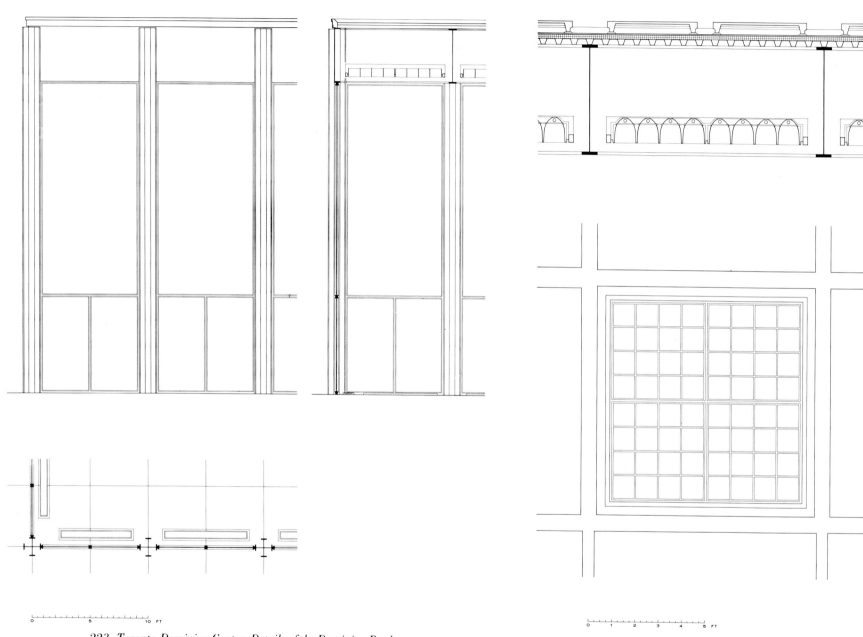

223. *Toronto-Dominion Center. Details of the Dominion Bank.*

186

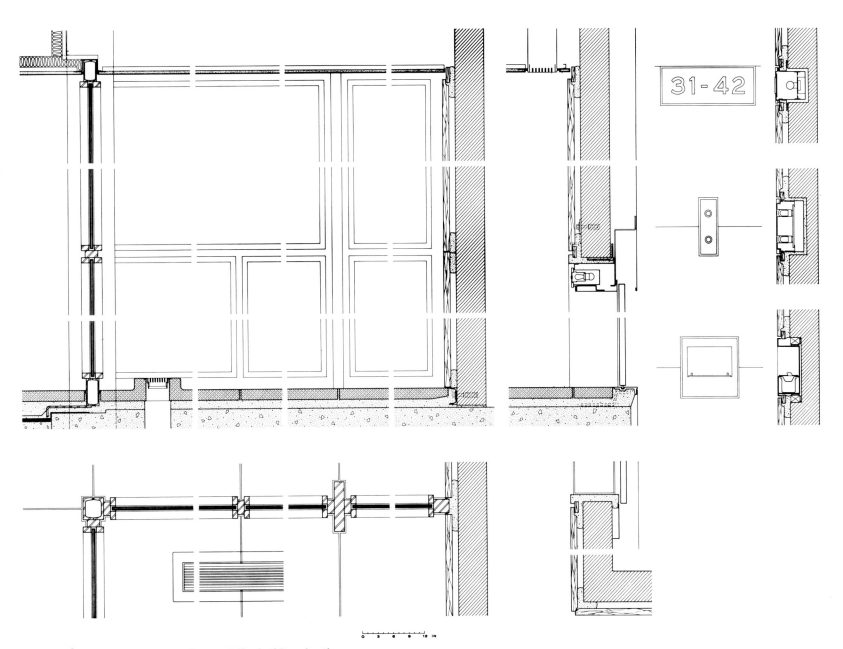

31-42

224. *Toronto-Dominion Center. Office building details.*

225. *Westmount Square, Montreal, Canada, 1965–68. Exterior.*

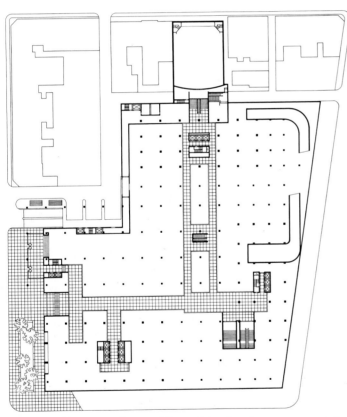

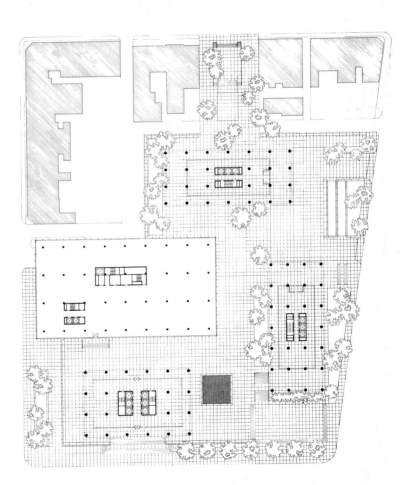

226, 227. *Westmount Square. Plans of the shopping concourse and plaza level.*

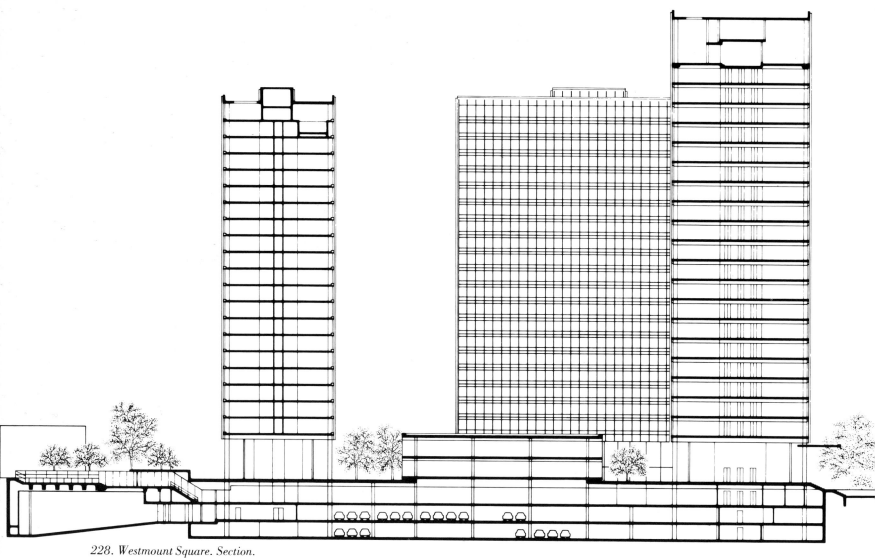

228. *Westmount Square. Section.*

190

229. Westmount Square.

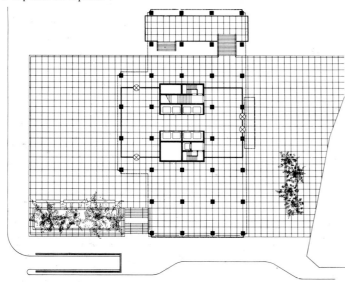

230, 231. One Charles Center, Baltimore, Maryland, 1960–63, and plaza level plan.

(1968); Dominion Square, Montreal (1968–69); and Northwest Plaza, Chicago (1967–70). Only one office building, the IBM Building, Chicago (1967–70), was constructed. This was Mies's last office building in the United States, and his last tall building in steel. In many respects it was also his best.

Unlike the sites for his other major office buildings, the site for the IBM Building was relatively small—slightly over 1½ acres. Easements had to be contended with as did restrictions as to how the site could be developed. The Northwestern Railroad had a right-of-way (below Wabash Avenue) which had to be maintained. The previous owners of the property, Field Enterprises, publishers of two Chicago newspapers, retained a portion of the site for newsprint storage.[7] And, as one critic noted, even the "neighbors" presented a problem.

"Directly west are Bertrand Goldberg's 60-story Marina City towers, twin exercises in sculptured concrete. And immediately east, the Sun-Times and Daily News Building squats seven stories low, a kind of bleached, World War II Victory Ship, fashioned out of aluminum, and complete with flying bridge."[8]

Mies's building relates well to its non-rectilinear neighbors. By placing the building, which occupies 50 percent of the site, well back from the Chicago River, a modest plaza was created, and complemented the adjacent Heald Square in front of the newspaper building. Bruno Conterato, one of the partners in Mies's office, described the reason for placement of the IBM Building:

". . . by going well back on the site, we in effect set up a line of three towers, since the Marina Towers are canted on their site, with the east structure farther north than the west one. This kept us from blocking any more of the view towards the lake than the east tower already does."[9]

It is a simple solution, obvious in retrospect, underscoring Mies's sensitivity to the surrounding environments.

The same concern for the environment is obvious in the

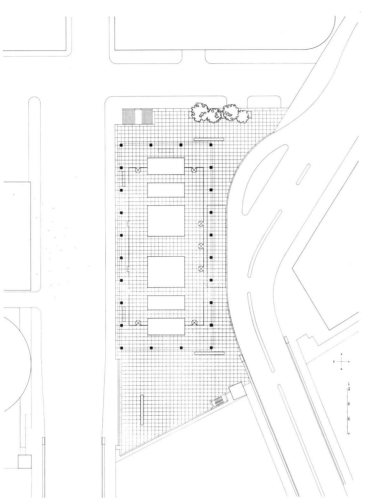

232. *IBM Building, Chicago, Illinois, 1967–70. Site plan.*
233. *IBM Building.*

solution for IBM's curtain wall. Here differences and re-finements are less obvious than are the similarities to curtain wall details in his other tall buildings. But the importance of this building lies in differences. IBM's curtain wall combined three elements used before only singly or in pairs: double glazing, a complete thermal break between the interior and exterior of the building, and a system to equalize pressure within the skin to prevent air leakage or infiltration normally caused by the pressure differential between a building's interior and exterior.[10] All these elements worked to produce a more efficient

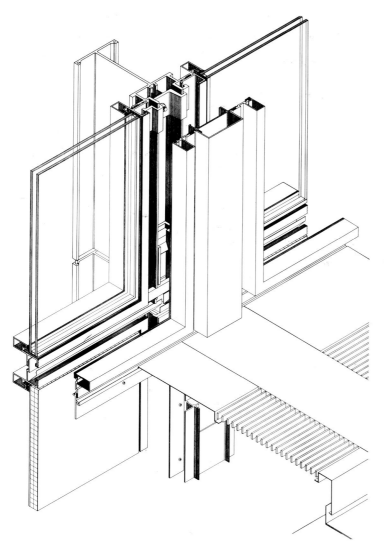
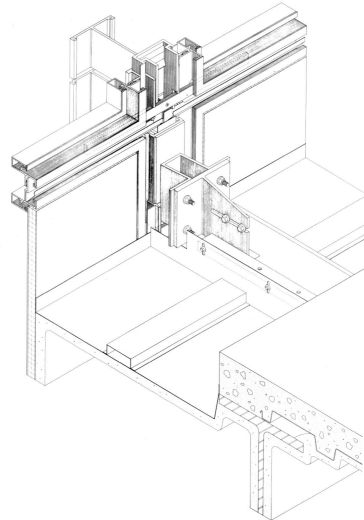

234, 235. IBM Building. Isometric drawings of the curtain wall.

curtain wall: there was less heat loss and heat gain in comparison with other buildings which had considerably less glass area.

With few exceptions, the impact of the larger urban complexes on which Mies worked during the 1960s overshadowed the smaller buildings of this period. This is true of three classroom/research facilities he designed for three different university campuses: the Social Service Adminis-

tration for the University of Chicago, Chicago (1962–65); Meredith Hall for Drake University, Des Moines (1962–65); and the Science Center for Duquesne University, Pittsburgh (1962–68). While all owe an obvious debt to Mies's work at IIT, each carries on his concern that a building has a clear, regular structure, that it be flexible, and that it implies the existence of a larger spatial order. This last aspect—the existence of a larger spatial order—is the most important contribution of these buildings to their respective environments. They stand as noble and singular examples of Mies's work on their campuses.

Four smaller buildings were constructed from designs Mies made near the end of his life, two of which were completed after his death. They are the Highfield House Apartments, Baltimore (1963–65); a second addition to the Museum of Fine Arts, Houston (1966–72); and the Martin Luther King, Jr. Library, Washington, D.C. (1966–72). There were also several unbuilt projects: a redevelopment scheme for New Haven (1966); the Church Street South School, also in New Haven (1966); Foster City Apartments, San Mateo (1966); and the King Broadcasting Studios, Seattle (1967–69).

Aside from its great size (330 feet long), Mies's second addition to Houston's Museum of Fine Arts is impressive for other reasons. Mies joined this new gallery to the existing museum with a skill and confidence made all the more remarkable by the fact that the new addition enclosed his earlier Cullinan Hall (1954–58). Cullinan Hall which had previously stood on its own as a piece of architecture now became a handsome interior gallery for sculpture in the final phase of the museum's expansion offering ample proof of Mies's consummate abilities as an architect: it was in his nature to solve the constituent parts of a problem as well as he solved the whole.

During his last years, arthritis and ill health prevented Mies from regularly going to his office. Frequently, his staff brought drawings and models of work-in-progress to him at home. In the comfort of his high-ceilinged, East Pearson Street apartment, Mies worked as he had always done—quietly, with deliberation and confidence. In spite of his physical infirmities, his mind remained clear, alert— his judgement unimpaired.

At eighty, in physical discomfort and with difficulty, Mies returned to Germany to attend the cornerstone laying ceremony for the New National Gallery. During this trip he was awarded the Gold Medal of the Bund Deutscher Architekten (Institute of German Architects). Returning to the United States late in the spring of 1966, he was presented the Gold Medal of the Chicago Chapter of the American Institute of Architects, and in June he received an honorary degree from IIT. Two institutions in his adopted city had at last formally recognized his achievements in architecture and his contributions to education, as other institutions, professional societies, universities and nations had already done. Mies did not deliver formal acceptance speeches on the occasion of either of his last two awards. However John Entenza, then director of the Chicago-based Graham Foundation for Advanced Studies in the Fine Arts, and long-time friend of Mies's, offered the following tribute at the Chicago AIA presentation:

"Almost six years ago, I stood here, and with several others, wished Mies van der Rohe a happy birthday. And now, I am privileged to participate in this presentation in which he will, we hope, honor us by being pleased to accept the highest accolade within the gift of the Chicago Chapter of the American Institute of Architects.

Under any other circumstances, and with any other man, one would approach this kind of thing with the recitation of a long list of accomplishments. But, after all, we are, hopefully, professionals, and I assume knowledgeable concerning the backgrounds of our great men. And besides, a recitation of victories, not only professional, but moral, might only shame those of us who had done so little.

It is all very well to honor a great man for the things he has accomplished, but it is also very important to be aware of the victories that were not entirely won: to know of the moments of despair when he must have been borne down by the small, incomprehensible stupidities of those who possess power without mind, vanity without substance, and greediness without honest appetite.

It is unlikely that any man can arrive at a moment such as this without some deep scar tissue, and we must honor him for his ability to withstand life, as well as for his major victories over it. And it might just be, that in the perverse nature of things as they are, a great creative man needs to function in this kind of boiling biological broth in order to refine and distill his attitudes about the real issues as he sees them. It is just possible that in some cases a solution is not really arrived at, as much as it is provoked. And no one can ever really know until the deed is largely done anyway.

There is no common denominator that can be used as a constant to check the superb balances necessary to this kind of creative tension.

Mies van der Rohe has accomplished so much so quietly that one wonders why other men have had to be so noisy. In my experience, I have never known silence to become so overwhelmingly monumental and charged with meaning.

In a day tending toward conformity, he remains a most singularly literate man, with an uncompromising rationale, who is too often embarrassingly too close to the truth. He has never asked to be forgiven anything. And he has shown an Olympian indifference to anyone who would presume to make excuses for him.

He has refused to speak when in his judgment there was nothing to say, and has permitted very little to be put down by way of characterizing material. I am sure, however, that there have been wonderful evenings of great unrecorded conversations, awash in a river of double Gibsons, and lost forever.

More than any major figure that I have known or heard of, he demands to be judged by his work alone. There are no ill-conceived judgments or personal furies, no public tantrums, little evidence of tension and doubt with which to mark out the geography of this great man.

Certainly there have been several of his contemporaries who have made great thunders as shakers and movers, in order to get the best out of their moment in time and place, but none of them have done all that he has done with his very special kind of surprisingly illuminating light; with a logic at the highest level of meaningful truth, with an intellect making its points so precisely that it develops a most exciting progression from fact to the inevitabilities of reason, and on to the exquisite balance of poetry.

And so, if I were a native of Chicago, I would want him to know how very grateful my city that he lived here, and for being not only a man fulfilling its greatest tradition, but also for being its architectural conscience."[11]

Mies continued to work for three more years. It was not until the condition of the cancerous throat tumor with which he had been afflicted for several years worsened and his health generally deteriorated that Mies was hospitalized. While at the hospital, he developed pneumonia and died August 7, 1969.[12]

With little ceremony, Mies was buried in Chicago's Graceland Cemetery, final resting place of many of the city's architectural leaders, including Louis H. Sullivan, leader of the first Chicago School. On October 25, 1969, Mies's relatives, friends, associates and former students gathered in Crown Hall for a memorial service. Those who were present did not mourn Mies's death as much, as they expressed their sense of loss—individual and collective—with his death. James Johnson Sweeney remembered Mies as a friend and recalled their friendship:

"Standing here in Crown Hall, with its scale that so appealed to Mies, I like to remember the first time I saw Mies van der Rohe and the impressions I had. It was in the spring of 1933. I had admired an apartment interior he had designed for Philip Johnson who had recently settled in New York. I was on my way to Europe and Germany on a business trip. Philip Johnson suggested that I call on Mies. I wrote him. He invited me to his office. When my wife and I entered, we both saw at once the answer to a question which had been troubling us for some time: Why was the Barcelona seat so wide? As we opened the door we realized Mies was seated on one and it just comfortably accommodated his breadth.

Perhaps 'amply' would be a more accurate word than comfortably. For we recognized something ample about Mies himself at that first glimpse—a quality which seemed related to everything about him, everything he admired, everything he did. The suit he was wearing was ample—

well cut to be sure, but easy on him—and of a sober rich material. The cigars he offered me, and smoked one after another, were likewise 'ample'—and of the finest Havana leaf. The glass and chromium steel table near which he was seated, which we had always thought strangely high in proportion to its width, now looked perfectly in scale with its designer. Even on that first visit, I realized Mies's love of space, scale and quality of material.

And thirty-three years later I was reminded of that first sight of Mies, when one evening after museum hours, looking for him, I happened into his Cullinan Hall of the Museum of Fine Arts in Houston and found him alone in that sparsely hung, white gallery—100 feet by 95 feet with a ceiling 32 feet high—once again on a Barcelona seat, again smoking a similar cigar, quietly studying that space he had so sensitively proportioned.

Another incident I like to remember was a telephone call I made to Mies in his apartment on East Pearson Street before rushing off to a plane. I had been in Chicago for the day for a lecture and was on my way back to New York. In my apologies for not having reached him earlier I mentioned something of the general subject of my talk, order and form in contemporary painting. 'Ah-yes,' he said slowly, 'Saint Augustine.' Nothing more.

Again I recall one Saturday afternoon in New York, happening to drop in at the Nierendorf Gallery. An exhibition was scheduled to be on view. To my surprise I found the gallery dismantled—or, rather, in the process of being dismantled. Mies was in town. And frequently he and his friend Karl Nierendorf used to take advantage of the weekend to clear the gallery walls of what was on view and amuse themselves in arranging a special exhibition of whatever they liked particularly, or wanted to see together from Nierendorf's stock. It might be a large selection of Nierendorf's best Paul Klees, of his Die Brücke pictures, or a single painting on a large, otherwise empty wall, a mode of presentation which particularly appealed to Mies.

Mies enjoyed this. He found it one of the happiest ways to spend a quiet weekend in New York. He loved Klee's paintings as he had liked Klee personally. He knew, perhaps better than anyone else, how to choose a Klee painting of quality. And it was from Nierendorf's stock that he built up the excellent group of Klees he had in his East Pearson Street apartment—Klees, Schwitters, and, what was always a surprise, a large Beckmann nude in his bedroom!

One has only to think of Mies' handsome 1942 drawing—and collage designs for 'an ideal museum for a small city'—to realize how much he enjoyed paintings and sculpture and his respect for them. In these projects one is hardly aware of the architecture. Where the presentation of works of art was concerned he felt that they should have complete priority. Architectural details, fantasies in installation or lighting that might even slightly distract the observer's attention from the works of art were inadmissible. The only features he permitted major demands were open spaces and a sensibility in its division. The relative 'absence of architecture,' as he put it, intensifies the individuality of each work of art and at the same time incorporates it into the entire design.

I remember his escape to New York ten days before the Cullinan Hall in Houston was inaugurated, distressed by the preparations for the first exhibition to be held there which he saw crowding the easy space he had envisaged for the Hall. And I recall his request for photographs of an installation of the same gallery sometime later when only three large paintings by Miro were hung, with a large Picasso oil and a monumental Chillida sculpture. He wanted to send it to Berlin with his project for the Berlin National Gallery. And he did so.

Space, amplitude and a comfortable relationship among the parts—unity, order, form—were his basic requirements. A lack of order in any part hurt him.

It is characteristic of the depth, complexity and subtlety of Mies's view of architecture that the man whose epicurean taste would wish to combine Roman travertine, Tinnian marble, gray transparent glass, onyx and chromium-plated, steel columns in his Barcelona pavilion and walls of striped black and pale brown Macassar ebony and tawny, gold-and-white onyx in his Tugendhat House could also declare with warmth and sincerity: 'Where can we find greater structural clarity than in the wooden buildings of old? Where can we find such unity of material, construction and form?—What feeling for material and what power of expression there is in these buildings! What warmth and beauty they have! They seem to be echoes of old songs!' This from the Mies we associate with the statement that concrete, steel and glass are the materials of our time and from these materials the forms of our epoch should evolve! But for Mies everything depended on 'how we use a material, not on the material itself'—'each material,' as he said, 'is only what we make it.' And Mies, in no matter what material he employed, as the bequest of buildings he has left Chicago bears witness, was essentially a builder. He never forgot his early lessons from his master-mason father. 'I learned about stone from him.' And I recall how pleased he was to recount the fact that as a young man—barely more than a boy—he had qualified as a journeyman bricklayer. 'Now a brick,' as he would say, 'that is really something!' 'How sensible is this small, handy shape, so useful for every purpose! What logic in its bonding, pattern and texture! What richness in the simplest wall surface! But what discipline this material imposes!' On this homely basis Mies established an unparalleled expression of new materials and engineering techniques: 'a form for an epoch.' Discipline, order, form: this was the progress he saw underlying the statement from Saint Augustine he was so fond of quoting. This, for him, in architecture, was Truth. Beauty was its splendor.

'All education,' he felt, 'must begin with the practical side of life,' but 'true education is concerned not only with practical goals but also with values. By our practical aims we are bound to the specific structure of our epoch. Our values, on the other hand, are rooted in the spiritual nature of men. Our practical aims measure only our material progress. The values we profess reveal the level of our culture—the long path from the material through function to creative work has only a single goal: to create order out of the desperate confusion of our time.'

And this is the bequest which Mies has left to all of us and particularly to Chicago: his vital, personal and inspiring patterns of order in a world which has suffered too long in recent years from the disregard of such a spiritual discipline.

Today there is no need to stress the value of Mies's contribution, nor his stature as an artist. As the latter, he had the good fortune to live to realize the universal recognition that was being paid him.

To the world he was a great architect and a modest, self-effacing man.

To his intimates he will always remain, what he always was to them, a benign monolith: a warm friend and full human being."[13]

1 "Affirming the Absolutes," *Time* 87 (February 11, 1966): 58.
2 "Royal Gold Medal for Architecture-1959," *Journal of Royal Institute of British Architects* 66 (July 1959): 308.
3 Ludwig Mies van der Rohe, [Acceptance Speech Upon Receiving the Gold Medal of the American Institute of Architects,] *Journal of the American Institute of Architects* 33 (June 1960): 90–91.
4 Arthur Drexler, *Transformations in Modern Architecture* (New York: The Museum of Modern Art, 1979), 4.
5 "Affirming the Absolutes," 61.
6 A. James Speyer, *Mies van der Rohe* (Chicago: Art Institute of Chicago, 1968), 84.
7 Rob Cuscaden, "The IBM Tower: 52 Stories of Glass and Steel on a Site that Seemed 'Almost Non-Existent,'" *Inland Architect* 16 (July 1972): 10.
8 Ibid.
9 Ibid.
10 Ibid., 12.
11 John Entenza, "The Presentation of the Gold Medal, Chicago Chapter, American Institute of Architects" (Graham Foundation for Advanced Studies in Fine Arts: 1966), 1–4.
12 According to Dirk Lohan, the immediate members of Mies's family and his closest friends decided to keep knowledge of the tumor from the public. So the official announcement listed the cause of death as chronic bronchitis coupled with pneumonia.
13 James Johnson Sweeney, "Tribute to Ludwig Mies van der Rohe," *Illinois Institute of Technology* (October 25, 1969): 1–6.

SELECTED BIBLIOGRAPHY

This bibliography has been arranged in the following manner: articles and speeches by Mies are arranged chronologically; these are followed by books and monographs arranged alphabetically by author or, if unattributed, by title, followed by journal and periodical articles arranged alphabetically by author or, if unattributed, by title.

Mies van der Rohe, Ludwig. "Hochhausprojekt für Bahnhof Friedrichstrasse in Berlin," *Fruhlicht* 1 (1922): 122–24.

————. "Bürohaus," *G* (Berlin), no. 1 (June 1923): 3.

————. "Bauen," *G* (Berlin), no. 2 (September 1923): 1.

————. "Baukunst und Zeitwille," *Der Querschnitt* 4 (1924): 31–32.

————. [Address to the 37th Association of Collegiate Schools of Architecture Annual Convention,] *Journal of Architectural Education* 7 (Summer 1951): 13–15.

————. "The End of the Bauhaus," *North Carolina University State College of Agriculture and Engineering, School of Design Publication,* 3 (Spring 1953): 16–18.

————. [Acceptance Speech Upon Receiving the Gold Medal of the American Institute of Architects,] *Journal of the American Institute of Architects* 33 (June 1960): 90–91.

. . .

Banham, Reyner. *Theory and Design in the First Machine Age.* London: Architectural Press, 1960.

Bau und Wohnung: die Bauten der Weissenhofsiedlung in Stuttgart errichtet 1927. Stuttgart: F. Wedekind, 1927.

Blake, Peter. *The Master Builders.* New York: Knopf, 1960.

Bonta, Juan Pablo. *An Anatomy of Architectural Interpretation: A Semiotic Review of the Criticism of Mies van der Rohe's Barcelona Pavilion.* Barcelona: Gustavo Gili, 1975.

Campbell, Joan. *The German Werkbund: The Politics of Reform in the Applied Arts.* Princeton: Princeton University Press, 1978.

Carr, Edward Hallett. *The Twenty Years' Crisis, 1919–1939.* New York: Harper and Row, Harper Torchbooks, 1964.

Carter, Peter. *Mies van der Rohe at Work.* New York: Praeger, 1973.

Drexler, Arthur. *Transformations in Modern Architecture.* New York: The Museum of Modern Art, 1979.

Fitch, James Marston. "Mies van der Rohe and the Platonic Virtues," *Four Great Makers of Modern Architecture.* New York: Columbia University Press, 1963.

Gay, Peter. *Weimar Culture: The Outsider as Insider.* New York: Harper and Row, Harper Torchbooks, 1970.

Glaeser, Ludwig. *Ludwig Mies van der Rohe: Furniture and Furniture Drawings; from the Design Collection and the Mies van der Rohe Archive.* (New York: Museum of Modern Art, 1977).

————. *Mies van der Rohe: The Barcelona Pavilion 50th Anniversary.* New York: Museum of Modern Art—Mies van der Rohe Archive, 1979.

Heald, Henry T. "Mies van der Rohe at I.I.T.," *Four Great Makers of Modern Architecture.* New York: Columbia University Press, 1963.

Hilberseimer, Ludwig. *Mies van der Rohe.* Chicago: Paul Theobald and Company, 1956.

Hitchcock, Henry-Russell and Philip Johnson. *The International Style: Architecture Since 1922.* New York: Norton, 1932.

Hitler, Adolf. *Mein Kampf,* eine Abrechnung, von Adolf Hitler . . . Munchen: F. Eher nachf., [1925–27] 1936.

Institute for Architecture and Urban Studies, *Philip Johnson: Processes [Catalogue 9].* New York: Institute for Architecture and Urban Studies, 1978.

Jacobs, Herbert. *Frank Lloyd Wright: America's Greatest Architect.* New York: Harcourt, Brace and World, Inc., 1965.

Johnson, Philip. *Mies van der Rohe.* New York: Museum of Modern Art, 1953.

————. *Writings.* New York: Oxford University Press, 1979.

Kliemann, Helga. *Die Novembergruppe.* Berlin: Mann Verlag, 1969.

Schinkel, Karl Friedrich. *Aus Schinkel's Nachlass: Reisetagebücher, Briefe und Aphorismen, mitgethelt und mit einem Verzeichniss sämmtlicher Werk Schinkel's versehen, von Alfred Freiherrn von Wolzogen.* Berlin: Verlag der Königlichen Geheimen Ober-Hofbuch Druckerei [R. Decker], 1862–64.

Schulz, Franz. *Mies van der Rohe: Interior Spaces.* Chicago: The Arts Club of Chicago, 1982.

Smithson, Alison and Peter. *Without Rhetoric: An Architectural Aesthetic 1955–1972.* London: Latimer New Dimensions, Ltd., 1973.

Spaeth, David A. *Ludwig Mies van der Rohe: An Annotated Bibliography and Chronology.* New York: Garland Publishing, Inc., 1979.

Speyer, A. James. *Mies van der Rohe.* Chicago: Art Institute of Chicago, 1968.

Tegethoff, Wolf. *Mies van der Rohe: Die Villen und Landhausprojekte.* Essen: Verlage Richard Bacht GmbH, 1981.

Willett, John. *Art and Politics in the Weimar Period.* New York: Pantheon, 1978.

Windsor, Alan. *Peter Behrens, Architect and Designer.* New York: Whitney Library of Design, Watson-Guptill Publications, 1981.

Wingler, Hans Maria. *The Bauhaus: Weimar, Dessau, Berlin, Chicago.* Translated by Wolfgang Jabs and Basil Gilbert. Edited by Joseph Stein. Cambridge: MIT Press, 1969.

. . .

"Affirming the Absolutes." *Time* 87 (February 11, 1966): 58.

"Apartments . . . ," *Architectural Forum* 92 (January 1950): 69–77.

"An Architecture Building for I.I.T." *Architectural Record* 120 (August 1956): 134–38.

"Architekt Ludwig Mies: Villa Des . . . Prof. Dr. Riehl in Neubabelsberg." *Moderne Bauformen* 9 (1910): 42–48.

"Armour's Architect." *Time* 32 (September 12, 1938): 50.

"Die Bewohner des Hauses Tugendhat äussern sich." *Die Form* 6hft11 (November 15, 1931): 439.

Bier, Justus, and Walter Riezler. "Kahn Man im Haus Tugendhat wohnen?" *Die Form* 6hft10 (October 15, 1931): 393.

Blake, Peter. "Ludwig Mies van der Rohe." *Architectural Forum* 87 (November 1947): 132.

Cadbury-Brown, H. T. "Ludwig Mies van der Rohe: An Address of Appreciation." *Architecture Association Journal* 75 (July 1959): 26–46.

Carter, Peter. "Mies van der Rohe, An Appreciation on the Occasion, This Month, of His 75th Birthday." *Architectural Design* 31 (March 1961): 95–121.

Cuscaden, Rob. "The IBM Tower: 52 Stories of Glass and Steel on a Site that Seemed 'Almost Non-Existent.'" *Inland Architect* 16 (July 1972): 10–12.

"Drawings for the Library and Administration Building, Illinois Institute." *Architects' Journal* 103 (January 3, 1946): 7–15.

Eames, Charles. "Museum of Modern Art Exhibit." *Arts and Architecture* 64 (December 1947): 24–27.

Entenza, John. "The Presentation of the Gold Medal, Chicago Chapter, American Institute of Architects." (Graham Foundation for Advanced Studies in the Fine Arts, 1966).

Genzmer, Walther. "Der Deutsche Reichspavillon auf der Internationalen Ausstellung, Barcelona." *Die Baugilde* 11 (1929): 1654–57.

"Glass House Stones; Farnsworth House." *Newsweek* 41 (June 8, 1953): 90.

Gordon, Elizabeth. "The Threat to the Next America." *House Beautiful* 95 (April 1953): 126–30, 250.

Hilberseimer, Ludwig. "Amerikanische Architektur." *G* (Berlin), no. 4 (March 1926): 4.

———. "Eine Würdigung des Projektes Mies van der Rohe für die Umbauung des Alexanderplatzes." *Das Neue Berlin* hft2 (February 1929): 39–41.

"House at New Canaan, Connecticut." *Architectural Review* 108 (September 1950): 154.

Huxtable, Ada Louise. "Legislating Against Quality." *The New York Times* sec 2 (May 26, 1963): 11.

"IIT Dedicates Crown Hall, New Design Building by Mies." *Architectural Forum* 104 (June 1956): 17, 21.

Johnson, Philip. "Annual Discourse 1979." *Royal Institute of British Architects Journal* 86 (July 1979): 328–32.

Kuh, Katherine. "Mies van der Rohe: Modern Classicist." *Saturday Review* 48 (January 23, 1965): 22–23, 61.

Lambert, Phyllis. "How a Building Gets Built." *Vassar Alumnae Magazine* (February 1959): 13–19.

"Metals and Minerals Research Building, Illinois Institute of Technology." *Architectural Forum* 79 (November 1943): 88–90.

"Mies' Farnsworth House Wins 25 Yr. Award." *American Institute of Architects Journal* 70 (March 1981): 9, 12.

"Mies Speaks 'I Do Not Design Buildings, I Develop Buildings.'" *Architectural Review* 144 (December 1968): 451–52.

"Mies van der Rohe: A Chapel." *Arts and Architecture* 70 (January 1953): 18–19.

"Mies van der Rohe Joins Armour Faculty." *Pencil Points* 19 (October 1938): Sup. 45.

"Mies van der Rohe's New Buildings." *Architectural Forum* 97 (November 1952): 93–110.

Mumford, Lewis. "Skyline: The Lesson of the Master." *New Yorker* 34 (September 13, 1958): 141–52.

Nelson, George. "Architects of Europe today . . . van der Rohe, Germany." *Pencil Points* 16 (September 1935): 453–60.

"Die neue Zeit: Schlussworte des Referats Mies van der Rohe auf der Wiener Tagung des deutschen Werkbundes." *Die Form* 5hft1 (August 1, 1930): 406.

"Presentation of the Royal Gold Medal for 1959 to Ludwig Mies van der Rohe." *Journal of the Royal Institute of British Architects* (July 1959): 304–08.

Read, Helen Appleton. "Germany at the Barcelona World's Fair." *Arts* 16 (October 1929): 112–13.

Ruegenberg, Sergius. "Ludwig Mies van der Rohe (1886–1969)." *Deutsche Bauzeitung* 103 (September 1, 1969): 660.

Schulze, Franz. "How Chicago got Mies—and Harvard Didn't." *Inland Architect* 21 (May 1977): 23–24.

"The Seagram Building Wins AIA's 25-Year Award." *American Institute of Architects Journal* 74 (April 1984): 22, 25.

"6 Students talk with Mies." *North Carolina University State College of Agriculture and Engineering, School of Design Student Publication* 2 (Spring 1952): 21–28.

Sweeney, James Johnson. "Tribute to Ludwig Mies van der Rohe." *Illinois Institute of Technology* (October 25, 1969).

ACKNOWLEDGEMENTS

When I began work on the manuscript for this book, I discovered that the process of collecting observations, opinions, anecdotes and facts had actually begun much earlier when I was a student. I was helped in this process of accumulation by four people who were, like myself, unaware that they were contributing to this work. I take this opportunity to express my sincere debt of gratitude to George Danforth, Howard Dearstyne, Ludwig Hilberseimer and Paul Thomas. In their separate and quite different ways as teachers and friends, each of them helped to shape the spirit in which this work was undertaken as well as contributing directly and indirectly to its content.

David Bielenberg, Juan Pablo Bonta, Mary Breeding, Mark Cordray, Diane Korling, Janet Isenhour, Walter Leedy, Robert Sexton, and David Vater deserve special recognition. Not only did they read the manuscript at various stages in its development, but they also willingly offered criticism for its improvement and encouragement to its author. This was not an easy task; I want each of them to know how much I appreciate their candor. Kenneth Frampton and my friend Edward Stanton deserve special recognition for the care with which they went over the manuscript, challenging assumptions, forcing clarification, and generally improving the work through their criticism. Each was a hard taskmaster, but the results were worth it.

To Georgia van der Rohe, Mies's daughter, and Dirk Lohan, Mies's grandson, I owe a debt of thanks. In addition to answering my questions, they provided me with useful background information which offered insight into Mies's personality and work. I am most grateful to Cheryl Akins for her unfailing good humor as she typed the drafts of the manuscript, and to Brian Clements and Anne Browne, my research assistants, who helped in the preparation of the citations in the manuscript and performed yeoman duties. For their assistance with the illustrations, I am deeply indebted to Victoria Behm of FCL Associates and Bill Tompkins and Rob Savage of Hedrich-Blessing Photographers: thank you for your generosity of spirit.

When progress was slow and writing painfully difficult, I am sure I tested the patience of friends and colleagues alike. I want to thank each of you for your consideration and understanding. When called upon to do so, I hope that I will be as considerate and as understanding.

D.A.S.
Lexington, Kentucky

SOURCES OF ILLUSTRATIONS

AP World Wide Photos: 214

Hedrich Blessing Photographers: 1, 2, 3, 6, 7, 8, 9, 10, 11, 12, 13, 20, 25, 27, 28, 29, 30, 31, 32, 33, 34, 35, 36, 37, 38, 39, 42, 43, 44, 45, 46, 47, 48, 49, 51, 52, 53, 54, 56, 57, 68, 69, 71, 72, 73, 74, 75, 76, 77, 78, 79, 82, 83, 84, 85, 87, 88, 89, 90, 91, 92, 93, 94, 95, 96, 99, 100, 101, 114, 115, 116, 117, 118, 119, 120, 121, 122, 123, 124, 125, 126, 127, 128, 129, 130, 131, 132, 133, 134, 135, 137, 138, 139, 140, 141, 142, 143, 144, 145, 146, 150, 151, 152, 153, 154, 155, 156, 157, 158, 159, 160, 161, 162, 163, 164, 165, 166, 167, 169, 170, 171, 172, 173, 174, 175, 176, 177, 178, 179, 180, 181, 182, 183, 184, 185, 186, 187, 188, 190, 191, 192, 193, 194, 195, 196, 197, 198, 199, 201, 203, 204, 205, 206, 207, 208, 211, 212, 213, 215, 216, 217, 218, 221, 222, 223, 224, 225, 226, 227, 228, 229, 230, 231, 233, 234, 235

Bill Engdahl, Hedrich Blessing: 4

Dr. Harold Bush: 5

Werner Blaser: 41

Howard Dearstyne: 55, 104

Courtesy, Howard Dearstyne's Estate: 50, 102, 105, 106, 107, 108, 109, 110, 111, 112

Courtesy, Philip Johnson: 147, 148, 149

Balthazar Korab: 209, 210, 219

Joseph J. Lucas: 168

Courtesy, the Mies van der Rohe Archive, The Museum of Modern Art: 59, 60, 63, 66, 70, 86, 97

Museum of Modern Art: 23, 62, 64, 65

Müller-Rentsch: 18, 21, 22

Fritz Schreiber: 103

Peter Smithson: 113

Ezra Stoller ESTO: 200

Ron Vickers Ltd.: 220

INDEX

Page numbers in italics refer to illustrations.